INSIGHTS
33 Lessons Learned
in
Medical Device Marketing

By: Timothy P. Walker, MBA

Life Catalyst Publishing

Cover design by COSMICDESIGN.
Interior Layout and Design by Lauren Nadler, Park City Publishing.
Trade paperback ISBN: 978-0-9976358-2-9

Printed in the United States of America

Dedication

This book is dedicated to all of my colleagues who have believed in me, invested in me, and followed me, for the first 35 years of my career.

You know who you are; I am humbly grateful for your support, I can only hope that I have served you well.

Preface

Now that I am deep into my career, it occurs to me that commercializing medical devices is difficult and is getting harder with every passing decade.

When I started on this journey in 1980, I didn't know how good I had it. Everything I was doing was a first for me, and frankly, for those around me. There were no books with helpful hints, advice, warnings; I truly had to figure it out as I went.

Wouldn't it be nice if there were a collection of stories that provided a starting point that you could build upon as you conducted your work as a medical device marketer? A perspective other than your supervisors that dared you to think differently and be bold, but provided you lessons that would allow you to avoid the pitfalls of inexperience?

This book is my humble attempt to provide that starting point and provide some hard earned lessons.

Please don't take this collection of stories as a prescription for success. If there is one lesson I have learned, it is that there is no one right way to do anything.

There are however, some better ways than others.

It is my hope that you gain what I refer to as a "golden nugget" of Insight from each of these stories and that those nuggets make your life a bit easier. Read the book through and then keep it close by as a reference for when you need it.

All the stories are based on real-life scenarios. Some of the situational details have been disguised or blended together to create complete stories.

As a further caveat, I have taken so many seminars and collaborated with so many professionals that I can't claim exclusive creative ownership over all of the content represented in this book.

OVER ARCHING PHILOSOPHY

I believe that an integrated commercialization strategy is necessary to create and sustain the success of all effective medical devices over the long-term. That integrated strategy is as equally important as the actual invention and development of the new product itself. This is even more true today than ever before.

So, Vision, Knowledge, Experience, Method, and Action, are all required to change the World of the clinician customer (launch a successful new product).

Core Beliefs...

I believe that

1. patient safety comes first and always.
2. the clinician customer is your most important guide, not King.
3. hands on experiences for customer input are superior to any mental exercise.
4. constant customer engagement in its many forms is the source of the product manager's influence and is critical to success.
5. minimal regulatory strategies never serve the good of the patient nor the product.
6. there should always be structure to the input that you are receiving from the field.
7. tension is natural and valuable between all stakeholders in the commercialization process.
8. going slow to go fast is the right approach, most of the time.
9. starting with the end in mind is the best way to ensure success.
10. you can't bring positive change to a process without being able to measure that process, never skipping a step or cheapening the ingredients.
11. practicing unethical behavior will never lead to success.
12. authenticity of purpose and action - to truly serve, is the best way to build important, lasting relationships.
13. multifunctional teams are required in the absence of true genius.
14. there are no limits to what is possible, only practical limitations that we choose to put on ourselves.
15. competitive analysis is often over done, it can dilute your differentiation strategies, know thy self.

Table of Contents

CHAPTER 1 MARKETING MANAGEMENT.. 1

LESSON 1   What is Marketing?

LESSON 2   The Marketing Continuum: a progression of activities and roles

LESSON 3   Market Development, "is it really different than Product Marketing?"

LESSON 4   Channel Selection Considerations for Getting your Medical Device to Market

LESSON 5   What Potential Acquirers Want Today in the Medical Device Market

LESSON 6   Building a Medical Device Marketing Team

LESSON 7   The Problem Solver Dilemma

CHAPTER 2 THE CUSTOMER... 25

LESSON 8   Voice of the Customer in Medical Device Product Development

LESSON 9   Creating Customer Profiles for the Medical Device Market

LESSON 10   Running a Key Opinion Leader (KOL) Meeting within the Medical Device Market

CHAPTER 3 STRATEGIC MESSAGING... 37

LESSON 11   STP Marketing Brings FOCUS to Medical Device Commercialization

LESSON 12   A Practical Approach to Segmentation in the Medical Device Market

LESSON 13   Important Aspects of Segment Targeting in the Medical Device Market

LESSON 14   Positioning Statement Development for Medical Devices

LESSON 15   Value Proposition Development for Medical Devices

LESSON 16   Hard and Soft Cost Reduction defined for Medical Devices

LESSON 17   Message Congruency in Medical Device Commercialization

LESSON 18   Social Media and Medical Device Marketing

LESSON 19   The Inventors Dilemma in Medical Device Start-ups

CHAPTER 4 PRODUCT MANAGEMENT 63

LESSON 20   AAPR – Annual Product Performance Review

LESSON 21 Conducting an Autopsy for Medical Device Launches that are Headed South

LESSON 22 Assessing Opportunities in the Medical Device Market

LESSON 23 State the Opportunity Size with Integrity, Medical Device Marketing

LESSON 24 Pricing a New Medical Device

LESSON 25 Be the Vision Keeper for Medical Device Product Development

LESSON 26 New Product Launch Planning: Topics for the Medical Device Market

LESSON 27 Writing a Great New Product Launch Objective for the Medical Device Market

CHAPTER 5 PRODUCT DEVELOPMENT MARKETING'S ROLE.................... 91

LESSON 28 High level Product Requirement Creation for New Medical Devices

LESSON 29 VOC input for Product Requirements Development

LESSON 30 Minimal Viable Product in the Medical Device Market

LESSON 31 Market Risk Identification in Product Portfolio Planning for the Medical Device Market

LESSON 32 Portfolio Planning in the Medical Device Market

LESSON 33 Goals and Objectives in Product Portfolio Planning for the Medical Device Market

ABOUT THE AUTHOR...113

ABOUT THE EXPERIA GROUP®, LLC...113

CHAPTER 1

Marketing Management

Regardless of the industry you are participating in, Marketing Management plays a critical role. You may find yourself managing products, portfolios, teams, campaigns, departments, or markets across the entire continuum of specialties within the broad category of Marketing[1]. In every one of these roles, you need to be able to take your strong academic background and learn to apply it.

The Medical Device sector of the Healthcare industry is filled with challenge, nuisance, heartache, frustration and an immense sense of satisfaction. This sector is not for the faint of heart, nor, for those prone to panic.

But if you love a complex, technical challenge where you will meet some of the most brilliant minds in clinical medicine and be stretched every day of your work life, then this industry is for you.

You must have command of the marketing process, own it and apply it in your company. You need to be the keeper of the grand vision at whatever level in the organization you find yourself. The more inclusionary you are in developing that grand vision the better it will be adopted throughout the organization.

This chapter is in no way complete. Each lesson has a golden nugget of information waiting for you. Each story was inspired by a question, observation, or memory.

Specifically, for the medical device market, I like to think of marketing as a Social Science. This is not your run-of-the-mill Business-to-Consumer market. It is not a Business-to-Business market. It is a Business-to-Clinical Institution market. Business-to-Clinical Institution marketing requires a level of integration between all facets of business. Central to all the integration is the Commercialization Process.

Even in a start-up environment, skipping steps, cutting corners and acting on unvalidated assumptions adds significant risk to your ultimate success.

Current trends that significantly impact this sector today are: increased cost pressure, a requirement for both clinical and health-economic evidence to prove value, and increased restriction brought on by regulatory globalization.

WHAT IS MARKETING?

WHAT IS MARKETING?

Have you ever tried to explain what it is you do and fumbled with the answer?

Explaining what marketing is to my father has proven a significant challenge. He grew up in a time when there was just "Sales". I often tried to use the famous Mr. Spock quote from Star Trek, the popular TV series, "The good of the many outweigh the needs of the few, or the one." The idea that Sales serves the one, Marketing serves the many. In a business-to-clinician (B2C) setting, sales and marketing are connected at a level that requires significant two-way communication. An interdependent relationship; neither can succeed without the other. Neither is first nor more important. Both are critical elements in the strategic marketing flow.

MARKETING DEFINED

For me, marketing is the "ethical application of applied psychology, with the intent of changing the behavior of a targeted group of humans." In our case, delivering a message in the "language" of the user that motivates them to modify their clinical practice, product choice or perception about their definition of value.

When I use the word "language" above, I don't simply mean the words, or even the media, that they are delivered with. I mean the application of a deep understanding, at an emotional level, of the target audience. That you thoroughly understand what makes the target audience, mad, sad, glad, fearful, hopeful and envious. Understanding the full gambit of emotions that your target audience experiences in their practice and letting that come through in your messaging helps you connect with them, making your messaging all that more persuasive.

Over the years, my father came to understand the difference between sales and marketing, almost. He now came to understand that sales and advertising are different aspect of marketing.

LESSONS

1. Commercializing medical devices require complete organization wide integration of action

2. Ethics matter, the ends do not justify the means

LESSON 2

THE MARKETING CONTINUUM™; NOT JUST ONE ROLE

THE STORY

I met with a recent MBA graduate that I found to be brilliant. This person questioned whether they could sustain the excitement that they felt in their first marketing position over a lifelong marketing career. My first question was, "why worry about it now?" Just enjoy the position. As we spoke it became apparent that no one had ever laid out the opportunities that the marketing continuum could offer him.

The Marketing continuum provides a tremendous variation of opportunity for you to ply your special talents. From corporate strategy to advertising, from portfolio planning to merchandising, from market development to product requirement planning, there is an opportunity for growth for everyone.

INTENT

What this story will do is define the continuum, explain some stages of the continuum and provide a tip or two about working within the continuum.

CAVEAT

Before I dive in, it is important to explain that the continuum is drawn left to right. There is not a hierarchy. Every role in marketing is equally important. There are several other continuums in most Medical Device

Companies as well. None are superior to the other. It takes a team to commercialize a medical device.

MARKETING CONTINUUM DEFINED

The marketing continuum is the progression of marketing activities that move from high-level strategy to tactical implementation of the business model. Marketing is the framework in which companies get intentional about their pathway to success.

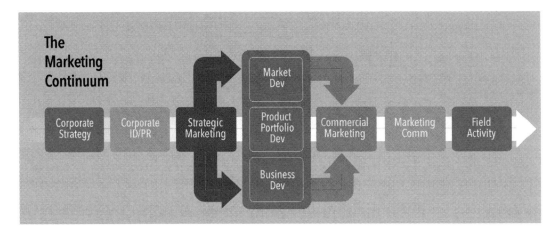

The Marketing Continuum

Corporate Strategy — Corporate ID/PR — Strategic Marketing — Market Dev / Product Portfolio Dev / Business Dev — Commercial Marketing — Marketing Comm — Field Activity

As shown in the figure above, there are seven areas of marketing contained within the continuum.

- Corporate Strategy
- Corporate ID/PR
- Strategic marketing
- Market development, Product portfolio development, Business development
- Commercial marketing
- Marketing communications
- Field activities

Corporate Strategy is included in the marketing continuum because to develop strong corporate-wide strategies many of the areas of expertise that marketers must possess are required. Without a marketing mindset, you cannot develop corporate strategies.

Corporate ID/PR is critically important and must provide an overreaching consistency with the product messaging. I include it to differentiate from the Market Communication role. Corporate Identification, i.e. corporate branding is a very different set of skills than standard marketing communications.

There are so many more customers for that type of message: employees, future employees, governments, investors, users and buyers, C-suites at your customers, etc. The messaging becomes broader and less specific.

Strategic Marketing represents the general overall positioning that an entire portfolio of products or services will be built around. It will define the opportunities for Market, Products and Services, and Business Development. Strategic marketing is often performed as a staff function, committee or senior management. Many times, too often, an outside consulting firm performs this function.

Market Development creates a larger opportunity, for the products and services by facilitating a new understanding or behavior in your current targeted group of customers.

Portfolio Development creates more products and services that act synergistically to penetrate market segments within the define market.

Business Development or M&A activities create new markets or provide access to technologies that power product and service development.

Commercial Marketing is critical to the success of the continuum. It is where the activities turn toward selling, training and building broader relationship. It is where the needs of the many are converted to the needs of the few or the one.

Marketing Communications is the process by which all the core messages are posed into a language, an image, a smell, and a feel all to trigger the desired emotional response from the customer. Once created these messages are then packed into different outlets or media types to reach out to the customers in an effective and efficient manner.

Field Activities, such as sales, clinical support, referral development, national accounts, customer service, product service, etc. has the task of taking the general messaging about the corporation, products and services and making it relevant to one customer at a time. Each customer interaction must be nuanced.

Having a marketing mindset serves you well up and down the continuum. The tools vary a bit, but the basics of marketing are the same in each stage of the continuum. I encourage you to work the continuum until you find your best fit.

After explaining the nature of the Marketing Continuum to this brilliant young product manager I could see his mind spinning with the possibilities for his future.

LESSONS
1. A marketing mindset has value throughout the organization
2. Experience across the continuum will be a good investment of

your time and make advancement in your career much more likely

---

LESSON 3
MARKET DEVELOPMENT,
"IS IT REALLY DIFFERENT THAN PRODUCT MARKETING?"

At a recent introductory meeting with a potential client I was asked if I had any idea why their sales growth was going so slowly. I had a little background with their issues so I explained that they were creating a market, not selling a product and that all their marketing efforts surrounded product sales messaging and activities.

He responded with the question in the title of this lesson.

At the heart of the Marketing continuum are three aspects of strategic marketing:

1. New Product Portfolio Development
2. Market Development
3. New Business Development.

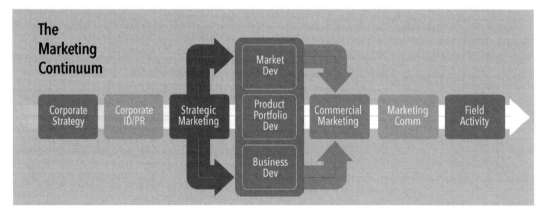

Are they different? Yes and No. To be successful in any of the three areas, you need a strong understanding of the core principles of marketing, a great understanding of your organizations capabilities and of course, a strong understanding of the nature of the customer and the environment in which they work.

The analytic tools you use are very similar. The basics of great messaging apply. Where they differ is in the nature of the problem you are trying to solve.

MARKET DEVELOPMENT DEFINED
Market Development is simply the creation or expansion of a market. To expand a market or create a market you must first "sell" the idea that a

problem exists. You need to educate the potential buyers that they have an unmet need that they were unaware of, or that was ill defined.

PRODUCT MARKETING DEFINED

Product Marketing, you are "selling" the solution to an already established problem or unmet need.

Typically, it is a very expensive and slow process to develop a market from scratch. There are many benefits in being the leader who creates a market. Typically, the first mover advantage provides leverage in the market place right up until someone develops a better solution.

On a relative scale, product marketing is quicker and less expensive than creating markets. See the figure below.

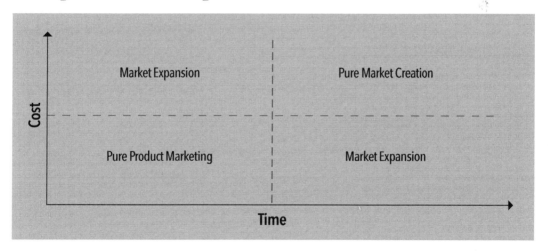

The client had a great product. There is a real clinical problem that this product solves. However, they had spent a large portion of their cash on selling a product to people who didn't see the problem. I was asked to provide insight into why they didn't recognize the issue and then fix it.

There are three or four "use cases" for this product. Some of the use cases are obvious to the key stakeholders, some aren't. The strategic marketing challenge is to find the balance between short-term sales and long-term market development.

It is not always obvious what to do. What brings the most success for the least investment? It is times like these, when you are facing complex strategic questions when I fall back on the core principles and tools of marketing.

1. When in doubt ask a customer(s):
   - Who is/are the buyer(s)?
   - Who are the key non-buying influencers?
   - Are the problem(s) that you are solving the same or different?
   - Is the product the right product for all use cases?
   - What are the barriers to success?
   - Is there a genuine value proposition for all stakeholders?
   - Is the value proposition strong enough to make it worth the user's time to be educated?
   - What resonates with the customers?
   - What evidence or proof will the buyer need to accept your proposition?

2. Scan the environment:
   - How large is each use case opportunity?
   - Is there competition or are you substituting an alternative solution?
   - Is there new technology on the horizon?
   - New laws or regulations that are coming or that are needed to provide leverage?
   - Are there any parallel examples of successful strategies?

3. Craft a hypothesis strategy:
   - Test your hypothesis
   - Model the potential results of your strategy
   - Select a strategy
   - Fire a bullet not a cannon ball[2]

There is no formula for crafting great market development strategies. You must eliminate the non-starters and then design tests to explore the ones you have hope for.

Despite increasing the number of implants by 300% per month with new strategies based on the real challenges they were facing, the investors chose to withhold the next round of financing as the company failed to meet their

2 Great by Choice, Jim Collins, Harper Business Press, Chapter 4, p. 60-98.

milestones.

LESSONS

1. Never cheat or skip a process step

2. It is Ok to go slow to go fast

3. Constantly check the metrics of success and don't wait to ask the questions if things are not going well

---

LESSON 4

CHANNEL SELECTION CONSIDERATIONS FOR GETTING YOUR MEDICAL DEVICE TO MARKET

THE SET UP

If you are in a large organization, usually you don't get an opportunity to be too creative about your go-to-market strategy. You probably have a process built into your quality system that defines the launch process. You have a well developed direct sales organization that is already in the field selling your products.

If you are in a start-up, a recent acquisition, or on a skunks work[3] project, then you may have more freedom to change the default channel.

If you have been in the industry for a while, it is only natural that you have bias about your approach to building a channel; there is nothing inherently wrong with using your default position. Unless of course you are wrong. Do the work and make sure the product will fit in your default channel.

Take a moment to answer the following questions:

1. Is the new product that you are readying for launch significantly similar to the previous products that drove the channel and process creation?

2. Is the company or target sales environment exactly the same as it was during the last successful launch? Competition? Reimbursement? Regulations? Customer?

3. Are the objective(s) for the launch of the new product the same as all the previous launches? Timing? Growth? Revenue? Impact? Value? Price?

4. Is top management pleased with the results from the most recent product launch?

5. Has your company effectively launched a product that faces the same channel challenges as this one? Practice development? Market development? IDN contracting? Complex referral patterns? Capital sales? The

---

3 Skunks works are projects that are not constrained by the current operational rules of your organization. One that requires secrecy, or speed that would be impossible in your current method of working.

need for service? A new type of value proposition?

If you answered YES to every question, then there is a good chance using your default position will be successful. If you answered NO to any ONE of the five questions, then it may be time to look at your default thinking or internal bias. If you answered NO to more than ONE of the five questions, then you should think through your default position.

"What worked yesterday doesn't always work today." [or tomorrow] - Elizabeth Gilbert.

THE STORY
I recently attended the Society of Interventional Radiology meeting in Vancouver, B.C. (SIR2016) and I saw many old friends there. One particular colleague and I had a rather deep and fun discussion about a decision that he made relating to the channel for a new product that he recently launched. Prior to the launch, we did not discuss his preference to launch a new product using a stocking distributor network within the United States. After experiencing quick initial sales growth for a year post launch, the growth crashed. His investors were initially very pleased as they saw quick, positive results; however, due to the crash they were now disappointed. He wanted a second opinion on what went wrong.

WHAT WENT WRONG?
To diagnosis what went wrong with this launch, we need a significant amount of information. Read, "Conducting an Autopsy for Medical Device Launches that are Heading South"[4] The issues always fall into one or more of seven broad headings: product, price, promotion, place, process, customer, or competitor.

The issue with this launch was place, the channel decision, and contributing to that, an unrealizable objective. We will explore what a good Launch Objective looks like in Chapter 4, Lesson 27.

This story identifies some of the key elements that need to be reviewed when working through the critical questions of: Which channel is used? and What is the right channel for your new product? I have created a worksheet table that I use to think through channel selection. The components that comprise the table are listed below with brief descriptions.

CONTROL – The more discipline that is required in message adherence, process and/or targeting of the selling organization the greater the need for direct control.

COVERAGE REQUIRED – This is a tricky one. Coverage requirements are

---

4 Chapter 4; Lesson 19.

driven by many variables: speed, geographical dispersion of the target customers, growth requirements, etc. This variable is very tied to the revenue objective.

EDUCATIONAL CHALLENGE –The more foreign the concepts are to the channel, the more education is required.

SPECIFICITY OF CUSTOMER TARGETING – The fewer customers that fit the target profile, the more laser-like your focus must be. More like firing a rifle as opposed to a shotgun.

DEVICE COMPLEXITY – Complex devices require a mastery by the channel such that the customer doesn't perceive them as complex.

CLINICAL SUCCESS – It goes without saying that repeat sales are a requirement, early clinical success is critical to ongoing sales.

VALIDATED MESSAGING – The more sure you are of the messaging, the more structured and prescriptive you can be in the sales training.

SALES-CYCLE DYNAMICS - Long, complex, sales processes that involve multiple influencers and are required to go to value analysis committees require a significant investment by the territory manager.

PRICE POINT – The higher the price, the more trust is involved in the relationship.

TYPE OF SELLING STYLE – Concept selling, missionary selling, F&B selling, commodity selling all require different skill sets.

Each of the above characteristics of the product or market aligns better with one of the seven channels.

What are the possible channels for US marketing of a Medical Device?

- Direct sales
- e-commerce
- Independent representative (agent)
- Stocking distributors
- Non-stocking distributors
- Strategic partner(s)
- Hybrid/combinations

For this story, the description of the market and product are as follows:

- Very simple product

- Very simple procedure
- Utility is realized by three stakeholders
- Product is purchased by only one stakeholder and they receive the least utility
- An emerging therapy
- Not too difficult to achieve clinical or technical success for the clinical user (learning curve is three supervised uses)
- Proven to be difficult to get repeatable results for those who receive the most direct utility
- Multiple influencers with above 20% influence
- Device cost in excess of $800.00 USD
- Reimbursement is available but does not cover the use of two devices
- Maximum single user experience in a 12 month period is currently 10 patients
- Concept sale required
- Messaging is evolving
- Long sales cycle (up to 120 days)
- The marketing process is a hybrid, with elements of both market development and product marketing

Explore the case described using the table to the right. See what you would have recommended and compare that with the decision that was made to use a stocking distributor.

Define a case that is relevant to you and see what you discover.

BACK TO THE STORY

So, what happened in my friend's launch scenario? He focused on sales and not usage of the product. He filled the stocking distributors channel and showed quick success. The stocking distributors were scoring a bunch of initial usages. He labeled them the "one and dones". The problem was that the initial users were not experiencing clinical success with the product.

So backing up in time, if we ask what was the challenge in selecting the "Best Fit" channel, it was that the Marketing Objective had a revenue target that was, in the mind of my friend, unattainable without 20 direct sales persons. He had been given a budget for channel development. The budget and the needed coverage were at odds. Instead of challenging the objective, he went for the largest coverage area he could within the budget he had been given. A stocking distributor model. He rationalized away that this product was a concept sale with a long and complex sales process. The

FOR YOUR DEVICE OR MARKET SEE WHICH TYPE WILL WORK BEST	TYPE OF DISTRIBUTION CHANNEL					
YOUR PRODUCT OR MARKET DYNAMICS	Direct sales org.	Independent agent(s)	Stocking distributor	Non-stocking distributor	Strategic partner	Hybrid
CONTROL	High level	Very low	Low	Very low	Depends	Depends
COVERAGE REQUIRED FOR SUCCESS	Scalable	Large	Medium	Large	Low	Large
EDUCATIONAL CHALLENGE	Large	Small	Medium	Small	Small	Large
SPECIFICITY OF TARGETING	Uncertain specificity	Very specific	Specific	Very specific	Low specificity	Very specific
DEVICE COMPLEXITY	High	Low	Medium - Low	Low	Medium - Low	High
CLINICAL SUCCESS	Difficult	Easy	Somewhat easy	Easy	Somewhat easy	Somewhat difficult
MESSAGING VALIDATION	Exploratory - Fully validated	Fully validated	Confident - Fully validated	Fully validated	Fully validated	Exploratory - fully validated
SALES PROCESS LENGTH	Long	Short	Mid-short	Short	Predictable	Long - Short
SALES PROCESS COMPLEXITY	Complex - simple	Simple	Predictable	Simple	Predictable	Complex- simple
DEVICE PRICE	High - Low	Low	Mid-Low	Low	High-Low	High - Low
TYPE OF SALE	Concept - Product	Product	Product	Product	Product	Concept - Product
NEED FOR CURRENT RELATIONSHIPS	High - Low	Mid	Mid-Low	Low	High - Low	High - Low

messaging wasn't validated. The targeting was not specific and it was difficult to achieve clinical success all the time.

Given this scenario, the obvious design was a Direct Selling organization. The time to have your investors embrace this is before you execute an alternative approach. Minimally, they have to hear your reasons for one channel over another. If they still direct you to use a lower cost channel model, then lower the forecast. Often, it is best to set up the alternatives before hand. For example: " If we go Direct with this number of TMs, our revenue curve is predicted to look like this." Or, "If we go with a Stocking Distributor network then the revenue curve will look like this".

Had he used the decision template, he would have understood that even though this was a simple product the other variables combined to require a Direct Sales model.

HINT: it cost $250,000 to bring on and train a Direct sales person. It takes even good TM's 3-6 months to be effective in a territory with a new product.

My friend went back to the Board of Directors and gave them a complete assessment of the state of the sales process using factual data. They authorized him to create a direct sales organization. Time will tell if they have enough money to make the change over. Strange how we can always afford to do things over but never seem to have enough resource to do it right the first time.

LESSONS

1. There is always time to think things through
2. Use a structured thought process to avoid bias and default thinking
3. Choose the right metrics to monitor your early success

LESSON 5
WHAT POTENTIAL ACQUIRERS WANT TODAY IN THE MEDICAL DEVICE MARKET

THE SET UP
Over the past two years I have had the good fortune to work directly with five medical device startup's. Through my mentoring and consulting work, I have also spent time with seven other start-ups, mostly medical devices companies

From that experience I have made several observations. A key observation for me is that being an entrepreneur is a spiritual journey. It is a calling that you can't hide from. It is also a journey that you can't take alone. No matter how broad your background is in all the disciplines of commercializing medical devices you still can't know it all or do it all.

Why? Because time marches on! The experience you may have gained in sales or R&D or manufacturing grows stale with time. What brought you success historically may not be what you need to be successful in the future. Your beliefs may be dated. I want you to succeed, so here is what I think you need to realize.

WHAT HAS CHANGED?
From a startup's perspective, in most cases, the days of bootstrapping[5] a finished product are gone. The need for high energy, high impact launches, and the capital to execute them, all but exclude slow rolling the launch of a new product. Why high-energy, high-impact

---

5 Minimum investment over a protracted period of time.

launches? It takes tremendous energy to break through the noise of the big players. Similar to the launch of a space rocket, it takes tremendous energy to break free of Earth's gravity.

Take a look at the following chart to see how acquirers have changed their expectations of potential device acquisitions over the last six decades.

DECADE	60's	70's	80's	90's	00's	10's	20's
SAFE PRODUCT STORY	X	X	X	X	X	X	X
SAFE STORY PROOF		X	X	X	X	X	X
IP			X	X	X	X	X
REGULATORY CLEARANCE/APPROVAL			X	X	X	X	X
CLINICAL OUTCOME STORY	X	X	X	X	X	X	
CLINICAL OUTCOME PROOF				X	X	X	X
HEALTH ECONOMIC PROOF (reimbursement)						X	X
SALES TRACTION BEYOND THE CHASM							X

Potential acquirers want all the risk removed. They only want to have to apply money and their high-powered sales channel to scale success. This means that you have to be prepared to take the device all the way through to commercial success. Commercial success does not mean that a few pioneering physicians have made it work; it doesn't mean that you completed your clinical trial. It simply means that you have an "equation" for successfully selling into the early majority, proof that you have leapt the chasm[6].

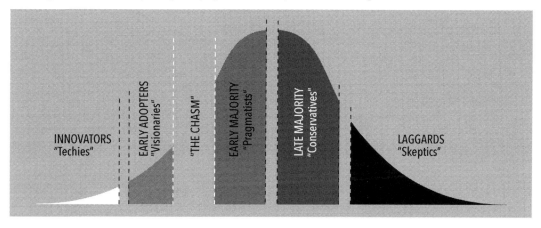

---

6 The Innovator's Dilemma; Clayton M. Christensen, HBS Press, Harvard Business School Press, 1997.

What are the components of the "equation"?

- Strong messaging (connects on an emotional level)
- Sales process that works (80% of the time)
- Believable value proposition
- Routine clinical success (utility is delivered w/o a lot of hoops or work-a-rounds)
- Clinical and economic evidence packaged professionally
- Satisfied customers who are re-ordering

WHAT HASN'T CHANGED?

Over the past six (6) decades almost every aspect of commercializing medical devices has changed. The aspects that have not changed are the core principles that I have referred to before.

- Engage with your customer
- Safety, safety, safety (no short-cuts)
- Quality, quality, quality (no short-cuts)
- Deliver complete utility with hard value
- Make the regulatory bodies your friend
- No single formulae for success, only guidelines

TAKE-A-WAY

In today's world of medical devices, entrepreneurs and inventors need to have a longer-term vision for their companies. The days where a patent, or regulatory clearance triggers an exit are all but gone. Too often the big players have not realized their hopes for gains from an acquisition. Often because success with a small sample of the market typically made up of KOLs and Early adopters does not translate to the Early majority.

LESSONS

1. Fund your company planning for the need to prove commercial viability
2. Bootstrapping is just not going to win in the 21 century
3. Success is still possible, just a bit more difficult

LESSON 6
BUILDING A MEDICAL DEVICE MARKETING TEAM

THE STORY
In two job assignments, my role was to build strong marketing teams. Both times there has been a nucleus of talent that were identified as "Product Managers". These product managers had a wide variety of knowledge, skills, education, background, and ability. Each manager was a valuable asset to the department; but only a handful had the classic marketing skills and education that one would seek in a prototypical Product or Marketing manager. The choices were pretty straight forward, 1) clean house and start from scratch, 2) build and develop the people you have on board already, 3) or some hybrid. In both roles, there was pressure from above to selectively clean house.

BUILDING A TEAM
Great marketing professionals come in all types of personalities, backgrounds, and education. In general terms, you need a person who is creative and disciplined, analytical and decisive, service oriented and focused, listener and doer. In short, you need a schizophrenic master of all things.

Alternatively, you need a very practical, aware, mature, talent-rich person who possesses all the tools that you learn in MBA classes. Or, you need a collection of professionals all who have unique skills sets that when combined give you a capability that leads to success.

In my experience, it is nearly impossible to find a number of prototypical marketers with which to build a team. Too many A-players can lead to disruptive environments. Institutional memory is too important to discount. In the medical device world, technical understanding, clinical understanding, customer relationships, and marketing skills all have great value. They are seldom present in any one person, at the start.

There are so many variables in building a team that it is almost impossible to account for them all, intellectually. Sometimes it just has to feel right. What I look for in a team member are the intangibles.

- Positive attitude
- Appropriate motivation
- Ability to learn
- Strong communications skills
- Situational awareness

The tangible aspects of the team members are that they must bring significant value. That value typically manifests in a specific knowledge or experience base and are more than likely surrounding one or more of the following:

- Technical knowledge
- Clinical knowledge
- Process skills
- Marketing skills
- Relationships
- History

If your team members bring value (valuable content) and have all the intangibles (core skills) you are likely to be able to build a team that will be successful.

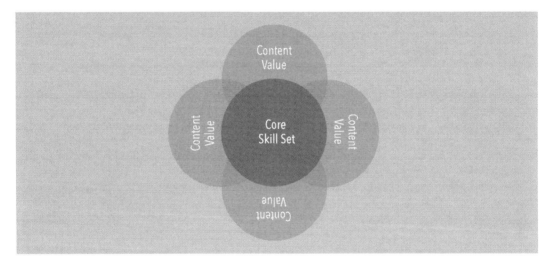

MY ADVICE

Set a timeline for yourself to evaluate the current team members in several different settings, say 90-180 days. Be intentional about that activity. Hold yourself accountable for personal debriefing sessions. If at any time you determine that a team member is lacking in one of the above five areas, or does not bring significant content value, start planning an exit strategy for them.

WATCH OUT

Make sure that your direct supervisor understands what your approach is and fully supports your approach. Evaluation over a 90-180 day period might look like a lack of leadership or decisiveness. Don't make that mistake; keep your chain of command fully informed.

MY ANSWER

A hybrid approach to building the initial team has been my choice every time. After the evaluation period, it becomes pretty clear who stays and who goes. It is not always clear when the change needs to happen. Do I think that cleaning house has a place? Yes, I do. Do I believe that building a team without any change to personnel is possible? Yes. If you do clean house, be prepared for significant disruption and long nights. If you don't clean house, be prepared for a slow patient teaching process.

In my career, I have only needed to make three (3) changes out of 60 inherited team members. By choosing to develop team members and letting them contribute the value they brought to the team I have accepted the responsibility to teach. Fortunately, or unfortunately I have a teaching gene.

LESSON

1. Respect the value of every team member
2. Keep your chain of command informed
3. Not everyone on a team needs to be a star
4. When you need to make a change, do it, but with respect and heart

LESSON 7
THE PROBLEM SOLVER DILEMMA™

THE SET UP
After attending a personal development seminar, I am a huge believer in continual learning, a realization occurred to me that would have been great to discover when I was managing large teams. So, I thought I would reveal my discovery in the hopes that someone out there will benefit.

THE DILEMMA
I discovered how much of my "self worth" was tied to solving marketing problems in the Medical Device space. Sometimes, I actually refered to myself as a "marketing engineer". Solving problems is what has led to many of my successes, so I don't discount the value of solving problems. I now realize that defining myself as a problem solver is self-limiting and can cost valuable time solving irrelevant problems. Knowing how to solve problems is a powerful skill to have. That is why I call it the "Problem Solver Dilemma". Solving the right problems, at the right time, in the right way, for the right reasons is a boundless way of receiving contributions to your self-esteem. When you are caught in the "Problem Solver Dilemma" it doesn't matter if the problem solving is contributing to the business imperative or not. A solved problem reinforces your self-definition whether it is the problem that can make the greatest contribution to the larger mission or not.

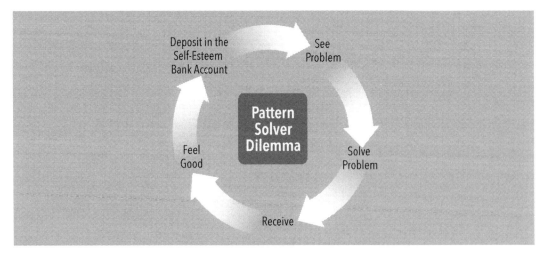

Have you ever thought that you were rearranging the deck chairs on the Titanic? The deck chairs probably were a mess and needed rearranging. But having orderly chairs would not save the ship or the passengers.

Reflecting back on my work history, my significant contributions came from seeing an opportunity to serve the larger mission (business imperative) in a new and creative way. Creating a vision surrounding that "new way" and effectively communicating the "new way" to others, who could help achieve the "new way" and then executing it regardless of opposition. I call this the "Vision Realization Loop™".

So how did I, or perhaps you, get caught up in this "Problem Solver Dilemma"? We forgot to ask several fundamental questions before we solved the problem.

WHAT TO DO

Once you have become aware that you, or one of your employees are caught in the "Problem Solver Dilemma" here is what you can do. Problem solvers need to be monitored closely. Why? They won't ask permission to solve a problem, they just start solving it. When this happens, it doesn't take long for a series of non-focused solutions to make a key resource in-effective with respect to their contribution to your greater vision or mission. They experience a series of satisfying experiences that leads them to believe they are being very valuable when the truth is, they are not contributing to the team effort. This is a disconnect that if not dealt with, "accidentally" creates a personnel problem in the future.

So how should I avoid the "Problem Solver Dilemma" before it becomes a problem? As this is a discovery that has just entered my conscious thought processes, I don't have a tested answer for you. But here is what I am going to do differently.

If you sense that you are solving a problem, stop. Ask yourself the following questions:

1. First, does this problem need solving right now?

2. Does solving this problem serve me or the greater mission that I am trying to support?

3. Am I solving this problem because I don't want to solve the real problem that would move us toward accomplishing the greater mission?

I have scheduled weekly meetings with myself (or perhaps with other team members) to monitor the problems that are being solved. I open each meeting by asking, "How does the work we have worked on over the past week directly support the goals of the company? What else have you worked on?" If the answers are not aligned with the assigned goals that directly impact the imperatives of the company, department, or project, then you need to honor the work, repaint the grand vision , and guide them to understand how their effort (though valuable) does not support the goals.

It is natural for you or them to make an argument that the effort does support the goal. Almost any problem that is solved can be indirectly related to the goals, however you are looking for a direct linkage. Listen carefully, they may be right. Either way, the discussion needs to end with a clear commit to realign their labor to support the bigger goal.

Weekly reflection time (weekly monitoring agenda)

- ◆ Review the "imperatives"
- ◆ Ask for a loose accounting of the preceding weekly effort
- ◆ Ask for a loose accounting of activity
- ◆ Honor the effort
- ◆ Check on alignment
- ◆ Repaint the grand vision (if needed)
- ◆ Let them or your inner self connect the Vision to effort
- ◆ Restate the future alignment

As perfection does not exist this realigning process is not a one time thing. That is why a weekly opportunity for reflection is important for everyone. Apollo 11 was off course 90+% of the time. Many small corrections allowed it to reach its destination successfully.

TAKE-A-WAY
The difference between the Vision Realization Loop and the Problem Solving Dilemma is that you are aligning your work with efforts that are serving the grander mission. If you can convert from just a problem solver to a problem solver who spends their efforts on moving the mission forward you will realize dramatic career growth.

LESSONS

1. Know thy self, first
2. Make sure that efforts are aligned with key objectives
3. Don't confuse progress (activity) with success
4. Problem solvers are valuable.
5. Solving the right problem at the right time in the right way is priceless

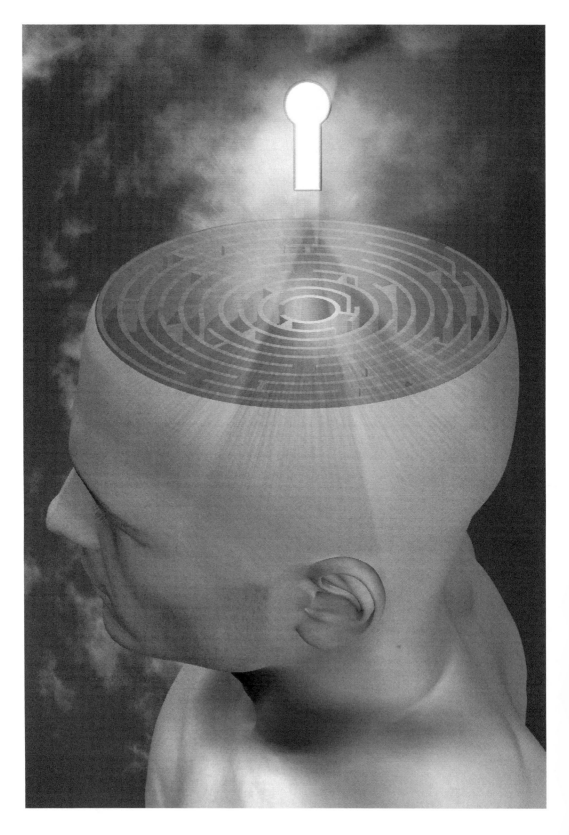

CHAPTER 2

The
Customer

At the heart of everything we do must be the customer. In the case of Medical Device Marketing the customer is a slippery concept. For me, the customer that I focus on first is the Clinician, second the "Care institution" and third is the Payer.

1. Clinician
2. Care institution
3. Payer

Why put the clinician first? It is a fair question and one that the answer to could change over time. For me, the utility that the device provides is derived based on a need, unmet need or latent need of the clinician providing the treatment for a disease, injury or trauma. If your product/device doesn't meet a need for the clinician, then none of the other stakeholders in the buying decision matter.

It is about Market Power. Who has the leverage? Revisiting this question often in your mind provides insight that others who might have lazy minds won't see.

Ask yourself these questions as a starting point:

1. Can a healthcare institution provide care without the clinicians?
2. Will patients and payers go to institutions without high quality care?
3. Who is responsible for the most important part of the customer experience, the clinicians, institutions or payers?
4. Can a clinician provide care without an institution?
5. Can a clinician earn money without a payer?

I am sure that there are more and better questions that you will develop over time, but start here. Until medical AI robots take over as our healthcare providers the clinician influence in the buying process will never go to zero.

Is the customer always right? No, absolutely not. Is the customer the right person to collaborate with to make sure you get it right? Yes, absolutely.

Do you have to consider other stakeholders in your input thinking? Absolutely. Just remember that your product will never get to a Value Analysis Committee (VAC) process without a clinical champion. All stakeholders are looking for value, as they perceive it. Whether they are the bio-medical engineer, the janitorial staff, the facilities managers, the inventory control clerk, the CFO, the risk manager, the PR department they all need something. If you know what that is and can frame your device/product to bring value to them, it is easier for your clinical champion to get what they want from the institution and subsequently receive reimbursement from the payer.

LESSON 8
VOICE OF THE CUSTOMER IN MEDICAL DEVICE PRODUCT DEVELOPMENT

THE SET UP

Over the past year I have been involved with a number of mentoring, coaching and consulting projects and one question that keeps coming up time and time again is: "When do I need to collect the Voice of the Customer (VOC) for input into my new product development process?"

TO-DO LIST:
1. LISTEN
2. HEAR
3. LEARN

There is a simple answer, which is, "all the time".
Now, the context and design contraints surrounding that answer are significant. In this lesson I will elaborate on the simple answer offered above. Hopefully you will gain from this perspective. Suffice it to say that regardless of the magnitude of the effort, it is one of the most important ongoing aspects of what the marketer does to ensure successful resolution of the problem in an attractive way.

CONTEXT

The way I think about VOC is that it is the first right activity to minimize risk of missing the mark with the utility of a new product. How much time and money you dedicate to the effort really depends on how well you understand the problem statement, how many unknowns there are, how different the solutions might be from technology they're used to using and how much of a change to their clinical practice might occur. In other words, how much design risk is there?

The age old concept of, "if we build it they will come" is not the case in Medical Device Commercialization.

There are too many preferences and nuances to believe that: a marketer, an engineer, an inventor, a single physician, could in isolation determine the right design approach for a device that solves a clinical problem and is attractive to the market.

As far as timing goes, the right time to begin collecting VOC is to test your hypothesized problem statement. Remember that you must determine if the opportunity is real? The, "is it real?" question is one that requires a deep understanding of the customer, their environment and the problem space. You need to collect insights through VOC to know if it is a real problem, how wide spread the problem is, and how accepted is the belief that the problem needs solving.

Once you understand the nature of the risks, I would recommend designing a customer input plan to parallel the design and development activities and make that part of your marketing plan.

For details regarding the VOC process itself see the Chapter 5: Lesson 29.

THE BIGGER QUESTION

The bigger question isn't when, but rather how extensive. The answer to that question is, "it depends." If the nature of the project is that its success is critical to your business, has a long development cycle or requires a huge amount of resources, then plan to get a significant amount of input before and throughout the development process.

If the risk is low or the technology is well understood, then maybe a customer input plan that involves fewer touch points or fewer physicians is OK. Just make sure that every stakeholders' view is represented.

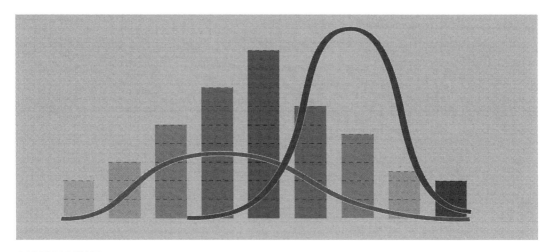

AN EXAMPLE

The project I am currently working on has six different types of clinicians in three different care setting that are targeted in the first 24 months post-launch. Normally, I would segment these groups out and prioritize their inputs based on the number or participants or by the dollar or unit volume that they represent. This time there is essentially no basis to prioritize the input.

For this project, I interviewed a high volume user in each category before I proposed a problem statement. That problem statement is tested with 10 inputs from each category or 60 physicians before I submit it to the R&D group for their concept generation process. I estimate that I will spend on average $500 per input and take six-weeks to collect the information. For the entire project (through technical design release), I am budgeting $240k- $360k that is used over a two-year period at different points in the process identified below. This may seem like a lot of money, it isn't. I have spent up to $1.4 million on a total VOC process.

Key Points for VOC

1. Pre problem statement development
2. Problem statement integration
3. Product requirement generation
4. Design concept ideation
5. Design concept selection
6. Design detail input
7. Clinical evidence plan input
8. Prototype utility study
9. Prototype human factors study
10. Validation protocol generation input

11. Design validation

12. Messaging input

Of course, this list is not the only time customer input would be collected. As mentioned in the first paragraph, VOC is collected all the time. The unique aspect of this particular device is that it is not intended for use internationally, reducing the complexity and cost substantially.

LESSONS

1. When in doubt ask the customer, not just one

2. Watch for bias in your sampling

3. Never stop listening

4. Risk-adjust your VOC efforts

5. Beware of KOLs (Key Opinion Leaders) representing the mainstream users

---

CREATING CUSTOMER PROFILES FOR THE MEDICAL DEVICE MARKET

THE STORY

The project I am currently working on for a client would have gone much quicker if I had followed my own advice and took care of the basics before creating final field facing messaging. I consider writing customer profiles or persona as one of the most important aspects of marketing fundamentals.

Once you have identified all the influencers in your buying decision the next step should be writing the persona. Without the persona you can't develop a segmentation or targeting strategy. Without segmentation and targeting you can't really develop positioning statements or value propositions. This is why the customer profile is a basic building block. Combined with your environmental scan you will have the fundamental inputs to developing the rest of the S-T-P marketing fundamentals.

CUSTOMER PROFILE DEFINED

A customer profile is a one-page document that describes the psychosocial aspects of your targeted customer group. Specifically, it will include the following elements: demographics, psychographics, behaviors, media preferences, influencers, preferences and environmental/ organizational constraints.

PSYCHOGRAPHICS

Are they anything like demographics? Sort of! Demographics explain "who" your buyer is, while psychographics explain "why" they buy. Demographic information includes gender, age, income, and marital status – the dry facts. Psychographic information might be their habits, hobbies, spending habits and values.

You can only effectively reach your target audience when you understand both their demographics and psychographics. The combination of both sets of data starts to form your buyer persona – a detailed picture of the people you work with now, and would like to work with in the future.[7]

WHY ARE THESE PROFILES SO IMPORTANT?

In a crowded field you must constantly look for leverage, something that will give you a leg up on the competition. Understanding your customers at a deeper level than competition will give you that leverage. It might lead you to align your product with a select group of customers. It might cause you to use colors and language that are more appealing. It might mean that you hire different types of salespeople. Even if you can't spend the market research money to do this exercise in a systematic method, it is worth doing! Treat the first draft as a hypothesis! Come back to that draft after every significant customer interaction to see if you have confirmed or rejected an aspect of your profile.

Here are a few simple steps in creating a good profile

1. Describe your customer
   ◆ Demographics
   ◆ Psychographics
   ◆ Behavior
   ◆ Language preferences

2. Locate your customers
   ◆ Where do they hang out?
   ◆ What do they read?
   ◆ What do they watch?

---

7 http://blog.hubspot.com/insiders/marketing-psychographics

- How do they learn?
- How do they communicate?
- Who do they admire?

3. Understand their buying practices
   - Where do they begin their research?
   - How do they receive the information they use in device selection?
   - What is their problem?
   - What benefits will you provide if you solve their problem?

4. Understand your current customers
   - Why did they originally buy from you?
   - Why do they continue to buy?
   - Why didn't they buy from you?

5. Write your first draft of the persona/profile
   - Write one per influencer.
   - Use names to give them life.
   - Look at the intersections for common elements.

TEST, TEST, TEST YOUR BELIEFS.
You must find a way to validate your persona. Market research is the obvious choice, unless you don't have the cash to pay for it. Then you have to use time and touches.

TIP
There is no such thing as an average customer! It is OK if you have to breakdown the persona into subgroups. I call these Archetypes. Your leverage will be greater if you find multi-modal conditions. Use of the mean/average is something that will lead you to being an average marketer.

LESSONS
1. Collect your input in a structured way
2. Customers persona can change over time, so re-validate your "rules of thumb"

RUNNING EFFECTIVE KEY OPINION LEADER (KOL) MEETINGS, FOR THE MEDICAL DEVICE MARKET

THE STORY

I will be running a KOL meeting this week and I thought writing this lesson would be a good way of capturing advice that I might give myself. I have been involved in bad, good and great meetings. Here is what I've learned.

Know what your objective is first. Otherwise, you end with, at best a fragmented process, and at worst an expensive party.

THE TOP TEN LIST

1. Bring value to the clinician beyond the honorarium that you are paying them. i.e. one suggestion is using a keynote address speaker on a relevant topic that is slightly off-axis.
2. Know what you want to learn before you plan the event or invite a physician.
3. Don't settle for narrative as the only input mechanism; get qualitative and quantitative data.
4. Recruit a physician to co-host the event. This brings credibility to the event as well as providing you a test bed for your structure.
5. Don't solicit advice on issues that you are unwilling to act on.
6. Work them hard; it communicates how valuable you believe their views are.
7. Comfort and convenience wins out over fancy and exotic every time.
8. Leave time in the schedule to let the physicians talk to one another without you present.
9. If you and they have the time for entertainment, make it memorable not expensive.
10. Themes are great for spring dances not so much with KOL meetings; don't go overboard with tying everything together.

MORE TIPS FOR SUCCESS

1. Logistics, logistics, logistics
2. A good rule of thumb is to spend 4 hours of planning for every one hour of meeting time.
3. Structure is important to good data capture; however, physicians will rebel against any structure that you might design. Accept that and make sure that within your structured discussions that you plan for unstructured time.
4. Conducting a pre-meeting survey is a great way to learn of dramatic

differences of opinion. Actually, using the slides from the survey is a great way to introduce controversial topics without it seeming as though you are trying to stir the pot.

WHEN TO UTILIZE PROFESSIONAL AND INDEPENDENT MODERATOR/FACILITATOR

I have developed the view that whether a professional moderator is used or a skilled facilitator from your own company is employed is dependent on a couple of issues:

1. What is the critical nature of the decisions I am collecting information to support?
   a. For high-risk critical decisions, I prefer a non-company based facilitator. It eliminates bias.
   b. For politically charged decisions I prefer an independent facilitator, it takes the pressure off the product marketer.
2. How many physicians will be attending?
   a. I don't recommend more than 10 physicians, however if you must go above 10 then a professional facilitator is preferred.
3. If there are several different physician specialties or a mix of clinician types then a professional facilitator can be helpful managing any accidental friction that occurs.
4. If you are going to spend the time and money to gather a group of physicians to help you resolve your critical issues, an additional $10,000 to have a coach or moderator make the chances for success go up dramatically.
5. Take the time to prepare a final report document that captures all that you learn and reveals the data organized by the data or findings that are associated with the critical questions you were trying to resolve.

TIPS IN SELECTING THE ATTENDEES FOR YOUR KOL PANEL

1. Select your attendees based on your objectives.
2. Make sure the invitees are representative of your target customer base.
3. Ensure that the physicians are still practicing physicians.
4. Don't send the invitations until you have vetted the potential personal conflicts or subservient relationships that may pre-exist.
5. If you "over-invite" to cover potential no's or last minute cancellation make sure you can handle the overflow if it happens. My approach is to nominate 30 physicians who all meet the acceptance criteria. Rank them. Invite 12 to get ten. If you don't get ten out of the 12, then extend to the next three people on your list. Keep rolling until you get your ten. This way you minimize your exposure.

FINAL THOUGHT

If you have never organized a KOL panel before, don't be stubborn ask for help. If there is no one in your organization that has done one, hire someone to help.

LESSONS

1. Logistics, logistics, logistics
2. Comfortable not swanky accommodations
3. Provide real value over and above honorarium

CHAPTER 3

Strategic Messaging

Strategic messaging is a huge topical area to discuss. This chapter has a collection of stories that touch on one of the core tenants of my personal Marketing Concept: Segmentation, Targeting and Positioning (STP).

The stories explain why I believe in STP marketing as a basic approach. For now, I'll borrow a line from the movie, The Patriot. Mel Gibson advises one of his sons that he should, "Aim small, miss small". Essentially, if you define the market or customer too broadly, you miss that portion of the market that really values the device/product that you are marketing. Couple this concept with the idea that to change a clinical behavior, you must generate significant momentum early in the launch process. It becomes pretty clear that in order to have early success, you need to be messaging the clinicians that receive the most value from the device/product.

Some of the lessons in this chapter contain analogies or metaphors that might be viewed as cruel or graphic. Hunting metaphors are just that, metaphors to help get across the point. Please if you are an animal rights activist forgive my expedient use of these examples in making my point.

Strategic Messaging is not about the final selection of words that you use with the customer or the words used to produce advertising copy. It is about expressing the core intent of the message. If you are an up-stream marketer or product manager your mission is to provide well thought out content based messaging.

Even if you are the person in your company that ultimately has to produce the final copy, don't skip the step of writing out the strategic message.

STP MARKETING BRINGS FOCUS TO MEDICAL DEVICE COMMERCIALIZATION

THE STORY
A couple of years back, I was leading a discussion with a group of Product Mangers about, "Getting the Message Heard" in the crowded arena of Medical Device Marketing. The group felt as though their product messages were getting over shadowed by the "Big Boys". They were complaining that to reach every physician in the relevant specialty they would have to spend an enormous amount of money.

The question I asked in return was, "why are you trying to reach every physician?"

I received several blank stares, a few chuckles, and a yawn. The conversation turned toward the power of FOCUS. My follow up question was, "When you are in a crowded room, say a cocktail party, how do you make sure you are hearing the person that you are talking with?" The responses: get closer to them, lean in, watch their lips to see if I can see what they are saying, isolate them in a quieter location, if it is important we leave the room.

The last question was, "what do all those techniques have in common?" The response: FOCUS. By increasing the Focus, concentrating our attention on the one voice that was important made their message and in return our message get through.

So what is the allegory in marketing? Segmentation, Targeting, Positioning (STP). STP Marketing is the thought construct that provides a vehicle for bringing focus, narrowing the beam, to those physicians who are most likely to want to use the device that you are preparing to launch.

SEGMENTATION, TARGETING, POSITIONING
For this lesson, I am just trying to introduce the topic. There will be subsequent lessons that go more into detail about each of these three elements. There are entire books dedicated to STP marketing and I encourage you to read them. The really cool aspect of STP marketing is that it can be used upfront in the new product development process to determine where the next right device opportunity is, or at the back end to focus the messaging of

a device that you have inherited.

When you think about STP marketing or if you are trying to explain it to a colleague or supervisor I use the analogy of hunting. Perhaps not politically correct but quite effective in getting the concept across.

SEGMENTATION - Identifying the part of the forest you should hunt in. Typically looking for habitat that is conducive for your desired prey.
TARGETING - Knowing the nature of your quarry to an extent that you are excluding large numbers of alternative quarries.
POSITIONING - Using the right equipment, bait, where to build your blinds, what type of call or decoy might be helpful.

PRACTICAL EXAMPLE

My first successful application of STP marketing was quite by accident. The device that we were commercializing was used to cool a blood-based mixture referred to as cardioplegia. This particular device utilized counter-current flow to optimize the efficiency of heat transfer. It also featured two other features. It had the lowest priming volume of any competitive device and it was easy to use once you had it set-up.

Segmentation – hospitals with high procedure volume (ease of use), a focus on pediatric surgery (low priming volumes), which believed in cold-blood cardioplegia, had an active PTCA practice (quick set up required), and was a teaching hospital (ease of use) (more likely to have University educated Chief Perfusionists).

Targeting – In those hospitals identified above, the probability of success went up dramatically if the Chief Perfusionist was a graduate of The Ohio State University Perfusion program. Why? Because on the final exam, there was a physics question, 'Which type of flow is most efficient when trying to remove heat from blood?' The answer, "counter-current flow." No selling or education was needed from the sales representative; they were already biased to believe.

Positioning – For perfusionists who are required to provide cold blood cardiolpegia in the most demanding of environments. The [device name] provides the most efficient cooling, lowest prime, and over all easiest to use system on the market. Utilizing a heat exchanger technology that maximizes cooling surface area, uses the most efficient exchange method (counter-current flow) all packaged in an innovative compact housing to minimize prime volumes.

The [device] went on to become the market share leader at a premium price.

STP thinking is not easy to reduce to practice with meaningful results. It requires a good deal of insight that can only come from unparalleled understanding of your customers. For me, Segmentation is always the greatest

challenge. To make it meaningful and differentiated from the competition requires a truly unique
perspective.

LESSONS

1. Look at who is accepting of your message
   and do a deep dive on why
2. Early success due to a narrow focus provides the momentum
   and learnings to expand beyond your initial segment
3. Insight is crucial

F OCUS
O N YOUR
C USTOMER FOR
U N-PARRALLED
S UCESS
™

LESSON 12

A PRACTICAL APPROACH TO SEGMENTATION IN THE MEDICAL DEVICE MARKET

THE SET UP

It just occurred to me that I had not completed the STP market trilogy. This
lesson will introduce the concept of segmentation, the S in STP marketing.
As a reminder the S-T-P in STP marketing stands for Segmentation, Targeting, and Positioning.

SEGMENTATION DEFINED

Segmentation is a methodology to cluster customers with similar buyer behavior (i.e., desired experiences, behaviors) into meaningful groups that can
be differentially targeted with unique marketing mixes.

Why should we segment the market at all?

- Segmentation can be a significant source of competitive advantage
- If you can "see" and "act on" a group of customers – that competitors
  "don't see" – you can quickly gain advantage
- If you segment the same way as competitors, you give up a very big
  potential source of competitive advantage

SEGMENTATION CHALLENGE

Of the three, segmentation has the most potential to set you apart in a significant way from your competition. Segmentation is also the most difficult
to do well. It's potential comes from the fact that you can segment a mar-

ket in a large number of ways:

- ◆ Geographically
- ◆ Technology
- ◆ Customer persona
- ◆ Customer type(s)
- ◆ Customer characteristic(s)
- ◆ Customer preference(s)
- ◆ Customer buying behavior
- ◆ Customer attitude
- ◆ Customer demographics
- ◆ Therapeutic method
- ◆ Care facility type
- ◆ Price point
- ◆ Distribution channel

The difficulty comes from having so many choices. How do you know which way is best for you? Difficulty also comes from the fact that you are likely to use multiple segmentation schemes for different reasons. The segmentation choice I am referring to here is to optimize your product based segmentation. In other words, how does segmenting the market help in defining or selling the product that I currently am developing.

SEGMENTATION SCHEMES

To select a segmentation scheme it must be: Meaningful and Actionable. See the table below for an example. Typically you would brainstorm the demand side variables and then score them with type of method.

		THERAPY X			
		ER	OR	Post-op	ICU
SURGEON					
INTENSIVIST	Physician				
	Respiratory therapist				
	Nurse				

EXAMPLE

For each segment you need to consider:

- Size?
- Competitive implications?
- How this might drive future success?
- How these might box you in?
- Is there a pathway for future growth?
- Is it possible to prioritize the segments?
- What are the channel implications?

LESSONS

1. Segmentation can help you see your customers differently than competition.
2. Segments must be meaningful and actionable.
3. Segmentation must lead to a targeting that works with your current sales force or be prepared to change it.

LESSON 13
IMPORTANT ASPECTS OF SEGMENT TARGETING IN THE MEDICAL DEVICE MARKET

TARGETING

Target as a descriptor is used in several different ways in Marketing. The Targeting that is referred to in this lesson is Segment Targeting. Targeting can't be accomplished until you have the Segmentation of the Market complete. As a reminder the S-T-P in STP marketing stands for Segmentation, Targeting, and Positioning.

◆ Targeting is simply selecting the segment or segments that will afford you your first right successes.

WHY SHOULD WE TARGET A SEGMENT AT ALL?

Ideally, your product or company would be equally appealing to the entire market. Seldom is that the case. To gain effectiveness and efficiencies, you target a limited segment which focuses your resources on the customers that you are most likely to be successful with.

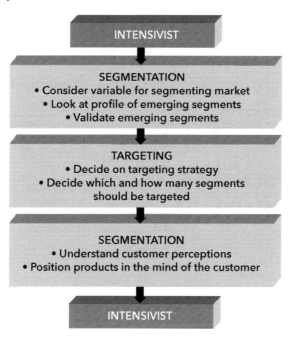

TARGETING CHALLENGE

The challenge with targeting is that it is a process of inclusion and exclusion. Very few sales organizations have reached the level of sophistication where they are willing to firmly accept exclusions. Honor this and leave room for deviation from your target. By leaving a little room for individualism for the sales professionals you will avoid an instantaneous negative reaction to a rigid set of rules and you will leave open a channel for exploration for secondary targeting or follow-on targeting.

		THERAPY X			
		ER	OR	Post-op	ICU
SURGEON		Leakage	Target	Target	
INTENSIVIST	Physician				
	Respiratory therapist				
	Nurse				

Leakage from your target segment into those you have excluded is unavoidable and in the long-term can be very beneficial, as long as it doesn't get out of control. So, in the example provided above, lets assume you choose OR and Post-Op vs. Surgeon as the target for your product. Trauma surgeons work in both the ER and the OR, there is some natural overlap. Or, let's say that your rep was scheduled in surgery and that appointment was canceled, they can go home or they can stop by the ER. Leakage can occur naturally or be driven by sales persons being opportunistic.

A real life example from my history is, that an ER physician presents at an M&M[8] conference and one of your doc's says, "in the OR we would have prevented that death by using this product, this way." The next day your rep gets a call from the ER doc that just experienced a death. How can you not make that sales call (perhaps the product manager makes the call)?

CRITICAL CONSIDERATION FOR TARGETING
- Is, or are, the segments large enough for you to reach your strategic goals/objectives?
- Even though the segments may have been differentiated enough in your segmentation scheme to be considered separately, are they similar enough to be combined?
- Does your product deliver strong utility to the target?

---

8 M&M - Mortality and Morbidity conference, held in most hospitals to review death or injuries that were possibly preventable.

LESSONS
1. Targeting is not about a single customer, yet
2. Targets must be large enough to be worthwhile
3. Targets must be able to realize the utility of your product or company
4. Practically, you will have leakage between segments

LESSON 14
POSITIONING STATEMENT DEVELOPMENT FOR MEDICAL DEVICES

THE STORY
Once during a staff meeting, the marketing team was discussing the portfolio of products that were under development. Of the Product Managers gathered at that time, five of them were preparing to launch new products and two were post-opportunity recognition and pre-requirements planning.

The discussion worked its way around to the realization that only one of the seven managers had formally written the "positioning statement" for their respective products. We bantered about the question of when should you write the positioning statement for the new product. There were positions voiced around the table that ranged from after verification testing, to after limited market evaluations.

Coming out of that meeting, all seven managers were given the assignment of writing position statements for their new products. Not surprisingly, over the next three days I was asked, what makes a good positioning statement? I was also asked, why one needed to be written at all?

WHY WRITE PRODUCT-POSITIONING STATEMENTS?
I have always believed, that the most enjoyable part of being a Product Manager was the early phases of defining a potential new product. No boundaries, no conditions, a clean sheet of paper, upon which you painted a dreamscape for your product. This is when you reach for the stars. This creative writing exercise, for me, often resulted in two-to-five pages of text and included a description of the clinical environment, the nature of the clinician persona, the problem statement, the perfect utility that the product could deliver, a forecast, a theme and never, never was restricted by the technology that was known to my company at that time. Very few of these stories have

ever been read or even seen by my colleagues. I used to think that it was a silly indulgence. What I now believe is that it is a critical aspect, which differentiates good new product definitions, from great ones.

What are marketers, if not the inventor of the story and the keepers of the vision?

Simply, we need to write the product positioning statement to concisely describe a vision to others, so that they can join us in making that story come to life. It is our elevator pitch to the organization and parallels the sales person's elevator pitch to the clinician customer. It is the executive summary of the multi-page story.

One real benefit to me has been that writing and telling the story imprints a vision of success in my mind and spirit. These visions of success often infect those around me, and instill a sense of confidence within them.

WHEN SHOULD WE WRITE THEM?

I think it is obvious that the product positioning statement should be written before the requirements planning process. The expense associated with research and other VOC activities is significant. You owe the organization a complete vision before you incur those expenses. If you can't generate some excitement with your vision then you shouldn't move forward, yet. Requirements planning reduces the grand story to something practical, that is tied to internal limits of resource and capability. The initial positioning statement never survives to the launch. Keep it current and revise it as needed. Always ask the question, "Is it still worth going after?"

WHAT MAKES A GOOD ONE?

For the first ten-years of my marketing career I didn't know what made a good positioning statement. I wrote good ones instinctively and mine were never consistent from product to product. At some point, I took a class and some really smart instructors from Stanford laid out a template. I use this template as a starting point for every positioning statement I have written since then.

There are seven distinct elements required for a complete positioning statement:

- Customer identification
- Description of those customer's problem
- The name of the product (preliminary)
- A basic description of the product utility
- A description of the components that offer the most relevant value (functional or emotional benefits)
- How it is different from competition
- Reasons to believe

FORMAT OF A POSITIONING STATEMENT

The statement is typically written as a single paragraph. I use two; however, your style can vary as long as you include the seven elements, can recite it in 15 seconds, and it tests as a strong statement. The paragraph typically follows the following structure:

For... . Who... . The... . Is a... . That... . Unlike... . It... .

EXAMPLE (COMPLETELY FICTITIOUS):

For the cardiovascular surgeon, **who** believes in the clinical benefits of beating heart surgery. **The** Squid **is a** combination rib spreader, retractor, and electrical isolation device. **That** offers maximum visibility and access to the heart, hands-free stabilization and counter traction, with the added ability to electrically isolate small areas of the muscle, all to provide a still and placid surface on which to sew. **Unlike** many devices on the market today that perform only one of these functions and do not offer an integrated solution to the problem of high quality stitching on a beating heart, such as the: [list competition here].

The Squid is offered by the leading manufacture of surgeon-focused equipment in the World today. **It** was designed for the unique requirements of the CV surgeon as directed by Dr. Spock, head of surgery at the Never-Never Land Heart Institute.

HOW STRONG A STATEMENT IS IT?

Test your statement against the following four questions:

- Is it compelling?
- Is it distinct?
- Is it achievable?
- Is it sustainable?

Have a group of independent marketers or better yet customers score the strength of your statement against the above four questions. Have them provide the reasons for their scores and then try to incorporate their feedback until an independent group scores you high on all four counts. Strong, average, poor makes a good scale.

LESSONS

1. Written product positioning statements bring clarity of vision to all involved

2. Make it compelling or start over - or cancel the project.

3. Test it with customers

4. Once you float it to the organization listen to all the feedback, you aren't the only great mind in your organization

---

LESSON 15
VALUE PROPOSITIONS FOR MEDICAL DEVICES

THE STORY
No story this time, I am breaking my format. As a reminder, the purpose of this lesson is to share experiences and lessons from a 35-year (still going strong) career marketing Medical Devices. Not all the lessons are directly applicable to every situation. At best, I hope you gain a "golden nugget" of insight that is helpful.

I received a phone call, after the pricing lesson, from a friend who asked me to layout my thinking on value proposition development. This is the response to that request.

REMINDER ABOUT VALUE
Value is the Utility of the device divided by the cost of acquisition plus installation or other switching cost – total resource savings.

$$Value = \frac{Utility}{(Cost\ of\ acquisition + Switching\ costs\ ) - Total\ resource\ savings}$$

What is a Value Proposition?
The value proposition is the step between the Positioning Statement and Pricing in the value development process. The diagram to the right is a little misleading in that it shows only one arrow. The truth is that each step is pro-

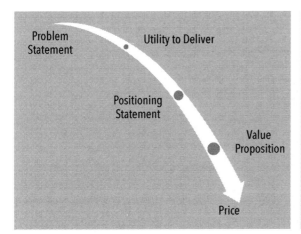
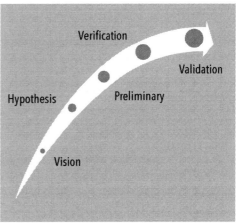

cessed through multiple times. First as a "vision", then they are revised to a "hypothesis", then they are revised once data is received as a "preliminary" plan, then once again after verification data is collected and again as after pre-launch market evaluations (validation).

Yes, I am sorry, that is five sets of revisions. Fortunately, the bulk of the work is done early so each subsequent revision is a matter of changing numbers or the priority of the features.

If you find yourself re-writing the value proposition every time you revise it, something is wrong with the original version.

The value proposition is the gross amount of economic benefit (expressed in words and numbers) that you will deliver to the user, the economic utility. As mentioned above, it goes through several progressively more "proven" phases of development.

SO HOW SHOULD I START THINKING ABOUT THE VALUE PROPOSITION OF MY NEW DEVICE?

The sources of value (utility) are not foreign or complex. Better, faster, cheaper, simpler, safer or access to new customer based revenue are the sources. Combining the sources of value is a great way to enhance your story. What can be very complex is, understanding the puts and takes of significant changes in the cost structure of the therapy with which the new device will be used. Even tougher is, proving that the value is realized in a specific hospital or practice.

HOW DO I START?

Start by creating a resource utilization map for the procedure that your device is used with. Find a friendly hospital/physician combination and follow the patient, with their permission, and write down, time or cost for every action, supply or RX used, from the time they are moved to the procedure suite until they are released to home, include anything they are required to take home with them. Map it. Cost it. Sum it. This becomes the source for your "vision".

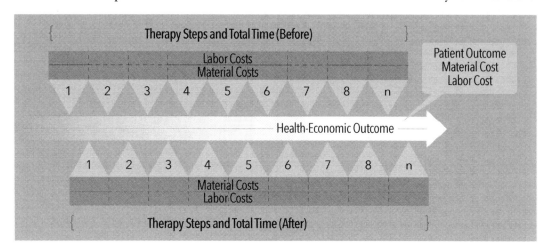

Ask yourself, "In a perfect world, how would the map change with my new device?" Brainstorm the possible sources of value. There are puts and takes (+, -). Pay particular attention to reduction in steps, reduction in meds, reduction in labor, and reduction in devices used. Also, pay attention to, increases in safety, increases in clinical outcomes, increases in resource utilization, etc.

Look at the resources used in accomplishing the therapy the old way. Then inject your device into the therapy map. Measure (theoretic) change through modeling. Then work to verify and validate those changes.

Find ways of proving the value is realized on a hospital-by-hospital basis. Test the map with different types of hospitals, rural vs. urban, community vs. university, teaching vs. non-teaching, large vs. small, etc. The most important facilities will be those included in your customer profile or your segmentation and targeting.

A GOOD TOOL

Now that you have the actual data, it is fairly simple to build a spread sheet based cost savings calculator. Having a tool that the sales professional can use to walk the materials manager through the value story is a strong way to customize the story and make it more real for the manager. If they give you their numbers to plug into a validated cost model it makes it difficult to argue the conclusions.

ANESTHETIC AGENT

	isoflurane	sevoflurane	desflurane
COST / BOTTLE	$17.00	$102.00	$74.50
% of use (total must = 100%)	0%	0%	100%

Number of Inhaled Anesthetics / Year	9,000	
MAC (Average)	1.0	
Fresh Gas Flow (averge)	2	L/min
Length of Inhaled Anesthetic (average procedure)	3	Hours
ANESTHETIC AGENT SAVINGS		
Total Premium Anesthetic to isoflurane Savings	$442,597	Per Year

OR TIME REDUCTION

Take Advantage of Anesthetics Agent Savings	Yes	
Time Savings	12,600	Per Year
Cost of / Minute (not including labor)	$29.00	
OR TIME REDUCTION SAVINGS		
Total OR Time Reduction Cost Savings	$386,400	Per Year

OR LABOR SAVINGS

Labor Rate	$50.00	Per Hour
Overtime Rate	$100.00	Per Hour
Number of OR in Use (not adjusted to TIVA use)	10	Per Day
Total Reduction in OR Overtime	$12,000	Per Year
OR LABOR SAVINGS		
Total OR Labor Savings	$21,200	Per Year

GROSS SAVINGS	$828,997	Per Year
QED-100 Cost (based on annual volume comittment)	$312,390	Per Year
NET SAVINGS	$618,807	Per Year

Material management processes within hospitals have become much more sophisticated over the past decade. They no longer "buy" a good story. They need to see the health-economic data to believe. Realized increases in value are considered hard savings. Those unrealizable cost savings that you include in your story are considered soft savings. Hospitals will hold you accountable for whatever value increase that you claim/promise your product or service delivers.

LESSONS

1. National value propositions don't always make a strong impact locally
2. Count on using Hard Cost only
3. Be careful not to over promise

LESSON 16

HARD AND SOFT COST REDUCTIONS DEFINED FOR MEDICAL DEVICES

THE STORY
I received a text, after the Value Proposition lesson, from a colleague who asked me to define the difference between Hard and Soft cost savings. This is the response to that request.

THE CONTEXT
From the Value Proposition lesson: "Material management processes within hospitals have become much more sophisticated over the past decade. They no longer "buy" a good story. They need to see the health-economic data to believe. Realized increases in value are considered hard savings. Those unrealizable cost savings that you include in your story are considered soft savings. Hospitals hold you accountable for whatever value increase that you claim/promise your product or service delivers.

HARD COST SAVINGS DEFINED
The Hard Cost savings are those resource utilization reductions that are tangibly realized. Such as, your new device does the jobs of three devices.

As an example,

(Price of device 1 + Price of device 2 + the Price of device 3) - The price of the new combination device = Hard cost savings.

($100.00 + $60.00 + $35.00) - $125.00 = $70.00 x 1,000 (the quantity of devices used) = $70,000 (realized cost reduction)

SOFT COST SAVINGS DEFINED
The Soft Cost savings are those theoretic savings that don't add up to a real reduction, or are those that may or may not be realized based on a probability, or those that might be saved by a department that is not in the same service line as the therapy that your new device is intended for.

EXAMPLE 1: Let's say that using your device will reduce OR time by 10 minutes per procedure. OR time is valued at a rate of $1,000 / min. Therefore, you tell the hospital that they will save $10,000 per procedure. This is a soft cost reduction. Why? The hospital has three OR suites that run concurrently. Any corresponding labor reduction won't reduce staffing. The timesaving isn't enough to do an extra procedure, so there is no increase in capacity. So, the likelihood that the hospital realizes the benefit, in a monetary sense, is low.

EXAMPLE 2: The national numbers indicate that a Serious Adverse Event (SAE) occurs for a procedure at a rate of 1/1,000 procedures. Nationally there are 100,000 procedures done annually. 100 SAEs per year. Your device reduces the probability of that SAE occurring to .1/1,000, so there would be 10 SAEs per year. The cost of that SAE to the hospital is $100,000. So, Nationally the cost of those SAEs is $10 Million dollars.

The hospital you are selling to does 500 procedures per year. The probability that they will experience an SAE is .05%, not very likely. The national story is solid but the local reality is that this is a Soft Cost reduction.

HARD VS. SOFT

Focus on the hard costs as a promise. The soft costs are bonus points, emphasis them in hospitals where they are more likely to matter. From example 2 above, if they are a hospital that does 10,000 procedures per year, or if they recently experienced the SAE they might be more inclined to see the benefit in the soft cost.

REMEMBER

This lesson only deals with the monetization of the value proposition. If your product doesn't add utility the cost of it doesn't really matter.

You sell locally, not nationally. Make sure that when you localize your story it still plays. As an aside, your value proposition may not play across borders. Don't assume, do your research.

LESSONS

1. Not all great national based value propositions translate locally
2. Don't over promise
3. Value propositions can also be based on revenue increases

MESSAGE CONGRUENCY IN MEDICAL DEVICE COMMERCIALIZATION

THE STORY

Have you ever seen messaging related to a new product that was clearly disjointed? Maybe you saw a tradeshow booth that spoke of the product a bit differently than the sales brochure and the salesman's pitch was a different story all together?

A VP of Marketing hired me to figure out why their dynamite new product wasn't gaining the momentum that they had expected. This is one of the most enjoyable and potentially beneficial services that I get to perform for clients. Consider it a launch autopsy.

There are many other causes for a slow takeoff of a new product. For this particular client, the issue was a confusing message. So confusing that one might describe it as conflicting. Why is this a big deal? As human beings, we seek congruency. We constantly are trying to connect the dots. The price must match the value of the product. The color schemes must represent the claims, etc. When our minds detect an incongruent message, we start to doubt everything about the issue or in our case the product. The customer loses trust in the product.

How do we prevent incongruent messages as marketers? There are lots of factors, but simply we need to know exactly what our message is, more importantly everyone that is working on or near the launch must understand the message.

HOW DO WE STAY ON MESSAGE?

We write. We publish the five core documents that then serve as the source for every piece of collateral, every training script, every creative brief.

- Segmentation
- Targeting (user and buyer)
- Product positioning statement
- Product value proposition
- Pricing strategy

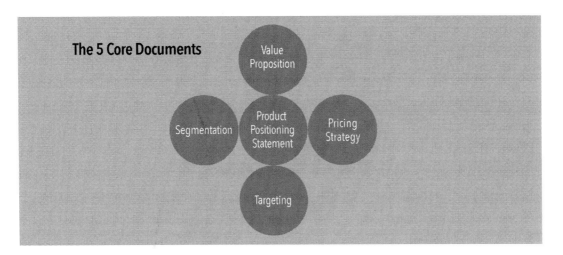

The 5 Core Documents

Value Proposition

Segmentation | Product Positioning Statement | Pricing Strategy

Targeting

THESE ARE THE FIVE DOCUMENTS THAT ACT AS THE BASE. EVERYTHING ELSE FLOWS FROM HERE.

In addition to these five core documents, there is a format to the story line. It is not mine; it is something that is adapted from other sources.

7 elements of the story

- Problem statement
- Reason to believe
- Proof set
- Solution statement
- Reasons to believe
- Proof set
- Call to action

If you publish the five core documents and keep any promotional materials and sales pitches in the seven-element format, it is unlikely that you will have incongruent or even worst conflicting messages.

LESSONS
1. Write the core messages
2. Communicate the messages clearly
3. Keep the language simple and in the vocabulary of the clinician

LESSON 18
SOCIAL MEDIA AND MEDICAL DEVICE MARKETING

THE STORY

A good friend of mine called me and started asking a lot of questions about the use of social media in medical device marketing. It seems that his VP read an article on Social Media and wanted an assessment of the benefit that it might have for their big product launch that is scheduled for 6-months from now.

We spoke for an hour and I truly felt bad for him. He interpreted his boss's question as an order to utilize social media.

KEEPING THINGS IN PERSPECTIVE

Social media is a very powerful tool. In and of itself it is not a goal. When someone tells me that they need social media I often ask, why? Not that I don't believe in the power of social media, I do, but if you can't tell me why you need social media there is a step missing. All marketing actions need to begin with a goal or objective, then a strategy to achieve the goal. Followed-up by a series of tactics to realize the goal aligned with the strategy.

THE STRATEGY IS CUSTOMER ENGAGEMENT

Customer engagement is one of those strategies that people label an objective that should be obvious to everyone, but it is not. It is well worth adding a section to your launch plan titled customer engagement, go into some detail about how, who, when, why the engagement will occur. Please remember to calculate the cost!

CUSTOMER ENGAGEMENT DEFINED

Customer ENGAGEMENT is a real time, active, two-way exchange of information, feelings and thoughts that afford participants to deepen their understanding of each other's needs, wants and desires. To further invest in each other!

"Consumer Engagement may be a broad topic, but it's the lifeblood of any sophisticated marketing organization's strategy. We define consumer engagement as the interactions between a brand and it's customer. These interactions can – and should – happen simultaneously across multiple online and offline marketing channels. Skilled marketers can guide this engagement to serve their business needs, while also providing consumers with an authentically enjoyable experience."[9]

If the right vehicle for that engagement includes social media or digital marketing then go for it!

METHODS OF CUSTOMER ENGAGEMENT IN MEDICAL DEVICE MARKETING

Customer engagement has been happening since the first medical device was invented. It is nothing new. It is ever increasing in importance and sophistication. There are new messaging channels and technologies for

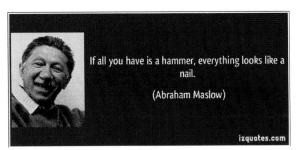

If all you have is a hammer, everything looks like a nail.

(Abraham Maslow)

izquotes.com

conducting the engagement. No one set of tools is optimal for any one market, segment, customer or product. You need to customize your plan. Don't fall into the trap of being a hammer, when everything looks like a nail. Choose the right tool for the job.

The following list identifies several engagement approaches:

- ◆ Key Opinion Leader involvement
- ◆ Speaker's bureaus
- ◆ Hand-on workshops
- ◆ Trade show events (training, contests, quizzes)
- ◆ Blogs that encourage feedback and discussion
- ◆ Chat rooms
- ◆ Panels
- ◆ Webinars
- ◆ Social media pages that are interactive

---

9 https://www.offerpop.com/definitions/what-is-consumer-engagement/

- Plant tours
- Direct consultive selling

Note that advertising, selling, telling, you-tube videos, e-mail blasts, Internet messaging are not on the engagement list. There is a fundamental reason for that as they are not two-way processes.

HOW DID THE STORY END?

My friend took a breath and reevaluated the launch plan. He added a section (3-slides) on customer engagement. He correctly identified that the broad based social media effort was not the right approach for engaging pioneers and early adopters. He did identify a strategic intent to capture the engagement with Pioneers and Early adopters and create an opportunity to "report" out that progression to the Early Majority users.

He added to his plan a tactic to create a private chat room (password protected, non-public access) for the "soft launch" users to exchange experiences with early use experience. Part of the plan to promote distance engagement was that every two weeks he would host a discussion forum via a virtual meeting room where engineers, marketers and clinicians could relate user successes and issues. I did recommend that a Quality representative attend to provide a real time assessment if a complaint needed to be filed and to record any and all clinical suggestions that might be proposed by an engineer.

An incredibly smart move on his part was to hire a digital marketing/social media, consulting firm to review the engagement strategy, and educate he and his team in where SM/DM might add value. Their mission was to optimize an integrated launch media strategy for the time that the "innovators chasm" had to be leapt and the early majority of the customer base needed to be approached.

Selling the expense for the consultant was easy. He presented it as way to increase the competency of his marketing organization, making sure that the tools available in the 21st century were appropriately applied.

LESSONS

1. Always start with an objective before designing a strategy
2. Customer engagement has many facets
3. Social media can be a powerful two-way communication channel to the customer; it is not an answer for everything

LESSON 19

THE INVENTORS DILEMMA IN MEDICAL DEVICE START-UPS

THE STORY

This Lesson may seem a little self-serving, it may be. But I celebrate everyone's success and feel compelled to sing out when I see inventors going down the wrong road. To some, the issue we are going to discuss is a bit of a chicken and egg scenario. I don't think so. It is more like the birth of twins.

I have been working with several early-stage start-ups {5} over the last several years {3} and have witnessed 15 'funding pitches', or more. I have noticed a trend. Those that get funding have strong technology, strong teams, some traction, and have real solutions to real problems all woven into a story that shows how they generate revenue (the business case).

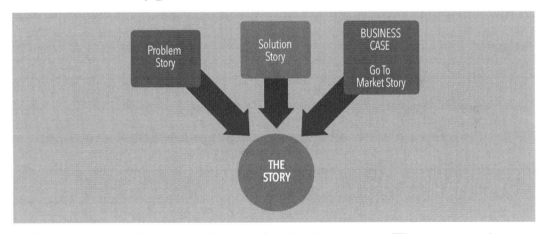

To an investor, there must be a viable business case. The stronger the case, the more solid the 'go to market strategy', the less risk is perceived, the more likely they are to invest.

I watch as these inventors 'pitch' their ideas and never deliver the punch line. How does this solution specifically make money? The second thing that is missing is an integrated commercialization strategy [the reason to believe that the solution can be delivered to the target market].

Passion and technology are critical, but they are not enough. Crafting an effective commercialization strategy and packaging it into a clean, understandable story is an art. It can't be formula driven. Yes, there are several outlines that the story can be organized into, but it is the connective tissue that links the story elements together. Humans make emotional decisions.

The investors must feel the value as much as calculate it.

There are several 'approaches' to telling your story. Lean start-ups, the Canvas, the five T's, etc. Many inventors get caught up in these approaches because they don't have formal business [marketing] training. They think that there is a formula for business success that is disconnected from their solution.

WHAT CAN THEY DO?

Developing that commercialization strategy needs to be done by a "professional" marketer. Yes, it costs some money. As a scientist, clinician, inventor it is baked into your mind that if you "build it they will come". The investors that you are presenting to are smart enough to know that it is simply not going to be that easy.

As an inventor/entrepreneur, you need to factor into the use of funds during the friends, family and fools or angel rounds enough cash to hire a professional marketer to develop a commercialization strategy that is plausible. At the very least, you need to have them scope the process that they would use to develop the story. A plan-to-a-plan. Find a good marketer and let them craft your story and determine the strongest go-to-market strategy.

LESSONS

1. Admit to what you don't know

2. Intelligence and experience are both required before insight happens

CHAPTER 4

Product Management

Of all the roles that I have held in Medical Device Marketing, by far the most rewarding were up-stream Product Management roles, followed by portfolio management positions.

Both roles require a technical/clinical/therapy understanding of the customers' environment. Lots of juicy details to immerse yourself in that require a closeness with clinician customers that other roles have not demanded.

This chapter tells nine stories, each one offering "golden nuggets" of wisdom that can be applied in your everyday tasks. This chapter provides insight that is valuable regardless of your specialized area of interests.

If you are a technical/clinical person either by training or experience, product management is a great entry point for you to become familiar with the marketing process.

Product management is the most emotionally challenging of the roles on the marketing continuum. In this role you have to be willing to say "no" to the "one", so that you can serve the "many". Great product strategy is exclusionary by its very nature. Two things my personality has a problem with, saying no and being exclusionary.

Hopefully the tools and lessons in this chapter will prepare you for being committed to the strategies you develop.

ANNUAL PRODUCT PERFORMANCE REVIEWS FOR MEDICAL DEVICES

One night, at 1:34 AM, I was awoken by a chirping smoke alarm, indicating that it needed to have a new battery installed.

After finding the ladder and the new battery, quickly making the change and jumping back into bed, I started thinking about how that experience paralleled my work history.

THE STORY
In the early 80's as a young product manager, I received a call from a production supervisor telling me that my biggest selling, most differentiated, oldest, product line was suffering from a 10% manufacturing yield and that I should get ready for significant, sustained back orders. I wasn't paying attention to my all-star product; I had moved on to more creative work. This is when I instituted the, "Annual Product Performance Review" (APPR).

DISCIPLINE VS. CREATIVITY
If I had only replaced all the smoke alarm batteries when I was supposed to, I would not have been shaken from a good night sleep. Discipline often escapes the truly creative person. As a product manager you need both discipline and creativity. One way to manage these sometimes-opposing attributes is to schedule the maintenance activities surrounding a downtime in your otherwise busy calendar. Never schedule them during sales meeting prep time, never during trade show season, etc.

ANNUAL PRODUCT PERFORMANCE REVIEWS, THE MINIMUM
I call this maintenance activity an APPR. As a product manager, we have to care for our product lines, particularly when they have been on the market for a while and the excitement of the launch has worn off. Spending one day a year, on each of your product lines is a minimal amount of your time invested that could prevent you from being shaken from a good night sleep by an overlooked issue. What kind of an issue? Quality shifts, pricing slip, share slip, new competitive entry, shifting sales force focus, slipping gross margins, resurgence, increasing complaint levels, all these potential issues are leading indicators of critical times for your product line.

The APPR can be done any time of year. At its core, is a year-over-year comparison of key metrics. The more years you have data for, the more likely you are to see a trend. It is good to partner with finance or IT the first time you conduct this type of analysis to make sure your data sources are complete and comparable. For some product lines a monthly review may be more appropriate.

Each APPR took a day and included a review of the following metrics:

- Units, total
- Unit, mix
- Average selling price (ASP)
- ASP by mix
- Complaint rate by type or category
- Manufacturing yields
- Gross margins (GM)
- Revenue
- Revenue distribution my geography
- Revenue distribution by sales territory
- Number of active accounts
- Number of accounts that went inactive over the past 12 months

These metrics are all loaded into a simple excel file, which automatically did the year-over-year trend comparison and some simple charting. The output was the APPR dashboard. Often this dashboard pointed towards areas that needed my attention and a bit of investigative work.

Today, I have created custom dashboards in salesforce.com that provides real time comparisons for new product launches. After one-year the dashboard changes to a periodic based trend analysis that has taken the place of the APPR dashboard. The important thing is to monitor the product lines you are responsible for and take nothing for granted. This is a good application of the, "productive paranoia" concept that Jim Collins discusses in his book, Great by Choice.

A HAPPY ENDING

What happened with the product that had the yield issue? After managing a yield of 10% and all the logistical and customer service issues that resulted, for over a year, a new manufacturing process was validated and up and running. The product was re-launched and regained 96% of its former share dominance. The product was just that good. The customers allowed us a second bite of the apple.

Since instituting the APPR, have I been shaken from a goodnight sleep by unanticipated product issues? Of course, the key being unanticipated – unpredictable or random issues.

LESSONS

1. Productive paranoia is a good thing
2. Periodic management reviews of all activity is a positive thing
3. Truth revealed in a positive way is powerful

CONDUCTING AN AUTOPSY FOR MEDICAL DEVICES WHOSE LAUNCHES ARE HEADING SOUTH

THE STORY

In lesson 17 I made mention of a "Launch Autopsy". When I first used this term, I received several inquiries as to what I meant. So here is the answer with a high level look at the process that I have developed to figure out, "what went wrong?"

The first product I ever launched went south. That was in the 80's. I was committed to determining what went wrong and what I could learn to prevent it from happening again. That is the first time I formally dissected the activities that lead up to a failed launch. I became a fan of "debriefs", regardless of the level of success that was obtained. A commitment to constant learning and refining of my skills was to become a hallmark of my life. If you're curious what went wrong with my first launch? The short answer, pricing.

A "Launch Autopsy" is the name that I have assigned to these debriefs. The name came from an article I read titled, "The Anatomy of a Good Product Launch". I figured if we have anatomy, we can have death and therefore an Autopsy.

LAUNCH AUTOPSY DEFINED

A Launch Autopsy is the formal process one uses to investigate an underperforming product that was launched within the past 12 months, it doesn't have to have failed (died) to have an autopsy performed (perhaps I should rename it).

WHY DO PRODUCT LAUNCHES NOT ACHIEVE SUCCESS?

Invariably the launch failures distill down to a "miss". A miss in the classic aspects of Marketing:

1. Product
2. Price

3. Promotion

4. Place

It might seem a bit old school, but it works. Each one of the four P's has additional levels below them. The 'what' is level one, the 'how' is level two, the 'why' is level three. It might make sense to think of Process as the fifth P. To modernize the thinking, I also add two Cs, customer and competition.

1. Product

2. Price

3. Promotion

4. Place

5. Process

6. Customer

7. Competition

I find that if you interview 5-10 key players in the launch, looking for the 'miss' in the seven categories' identified above, you can write a good hypothesis to explain what went wrong.

BEWARE THE MOTIVES
If this process is to be used to conduct a witch-hunt it will fail to deliver an optimized result. If the goal is to genuinely figure out what went wrong, then it can be a great learning experience for the organization and improves future launches.

A High Level View of the Process

1. Read the Quality manual – understand the Quality System well

2. Scan the DHF paying close attention to the customer inputs (VOC)

3. Interview the Product Manager and their supervisor

4. Interview the person that initiates the autopsy

5. Interview the top sales person

6. Interview the best historic salesperson who has not done well with this product

7. Interview the clinician customer that has bought the most

8. Interview the clinician customer who evaluated it and chose not to purchase

9. Develop a hypothesis or two that fit the puzzle pieces together

10. Test the hypothesis

11. Draw your conclusion(s) and present the findings

LESSONS

1. Pull on every loose thread that you discover
2. Focus on the blocking and tackling
3. Note but don't focus on the names
4. Focus on the process of the work and the content quality

LESSON 22
ASSESSING OPPORTUNITIES IN THE MEDICAL DEVICE MARKET

THE STORY

I attended a recent Medical Device investor conference and was approached by a colleague who had been following my blog for a year or so. I've known this gentleman for over 20-years, but had not spoken with him in quite a while. He asked when I was going to lesson something about doing Opportunity Assessments.

It is funny how people pigeonhole you into different skill sets. He remembered a Market Assessment I had done in the 90's that apparently impressed him. I have done so many assessments, both Product and Market that I had to look it up. I was humbled by the fact he remembered it.

A second gentleman that was at this same conference remembered me for the way I developed a Product Portfolio, he asked when I was going to blog about that topic. Again, I was humbled. This guy is as sharp as they come.

Both topics are huge in scope. In this lesson l set up some thoughts and definitions.

OPPORTUNITY ASSESSMENT DEFINED

An opportunity assessment is the systematic, fact based, analysis of the market and/or product variables and assumptions that are used to determine the future financial viability of a given "Opportunity".

PORTFOLIO PLAN DEFINED

The Portfolio Plan is the result of a systematic decision-making process that combines a series of investment options (opportunities) into a strategic investment across time. When the opportunities are combined, they will optimize that investment against a strategic objective set forth by Sr. management, hopefully that came out of a formal strategic planning process.

CONNECTING OPPORTUNITY ASSESSMENTS AND PORTFOLIO PLANNING

You can create an Opportunity Assessment completely independently of portfolio considerations. But to do a serious Portfolio Plan you can't do it without a series of valid Opportunity Assessments. To facilitate a defendable Portfolio Plan you must make sure that the methodology used to develop the Opportunity Assessments is consistent and not based on opinion.

Even if your organization uses M&A activity to build the Portfolio you still need that Opportunity Assessment. You might just call it Due Diligence. Take care to ensure that all departments use the same Opportunity assessment rules and validation requirements.

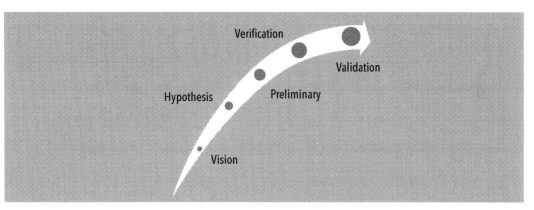

Depending on how your organization is structured, you will more than likely need to build the assessment in tiers of certainty. Some of the work takes resources and if you don't have the resources you need then you will need to convince someone that the opportunity is worth looking into. Think about the following flow:

- ◆ Vision
- ◆ Hypothesis
- ◆ Preliminary
- ◆ Verification
- ◆ Validation

WHAT DOES A GOOD OPPORTUNITY ASSESSMENT LOOK LIKE?

It all starts with defining a problem in a specific therapeutic area or market. Opportunity identification is a whole different topic. For this example, I will assume that the problem has been identified.

So the key questions that must be answered are:

- ◆ Is the opportunity real?

- ◆ Is it worth going after?
- ◆ Can your company win, if they go after it?

A NO to any of these basic three questions suggests that it is not viable, for you. Of course, everything has many shades of gray and all assessments are nuanced by political, economic and time frame realities. I will write from a simplified dogmatic position. Take it for what it is worth to you.

IS THE OPPORTUNITY REAL?

There are two parts to this question. Is the problem real? Is the solution real? To answer these questions, you must have a clear understanding of the unmet need. You must also have a reasonable belief that full utility can be delivered via the final product design at a cost that is affordable.

A mistake that often occurs is that someone sees a problem and assumes that everyone must see, have, or suffer from the problem. This is seldom the case. A measured assessment of the size of the opportunity is step one.

In almost all cases the problems are already being solved or mitigated today, somehow, to some extent. Don't discount the value of understanding how this happens. In a latent need these substitution solutions maybe your largest competitive hurdle.

IS IT WORTH IT?

This is a unique question that each organization answers differently. Depending on your grand objectives that have come down from the Strategic Plan, there may be hurdle rates that must be met even to be considered as a viable opportunity to be considered.

In general, this is a financial/strategic question that requires several models and market/segment/solution assumptions to be made. The more informed these assumptions are, the better the models are.

Typical you will need:

- ◆ A disease model
- ◆ A market model
- ◆ A set of explicit solution assumptions (validated to your comfort level)
- ◆ A set of explicit market assumptions (validated to your comfort level)
- ◆ A set of assumptions about the success of your product solution (validated to your comfort level)
- ◆ Cost of developing the product

- Cost of launching the product
- Sensitivity analysis of the revenue and profit models
- A discount factor is developed (probability of success on all fronts) (project ßeta)
- A pricing model
- A business model to deliver long-term success
- NPV
- IRR
- Payback period
- Strategic value (risk reduction, critical growth objective, etc.)

If, you are going to use this as one of the opportunity assessments in your portfolio planning process, then there needs to be a preset standard quality level for validation of assumptions.

CAN YOU WIN?

This question is primarily an assessment of your internal capabilities and resources. Some of these questions feedback to the "worth it" question. For example, if you need to acquire or invent a new technology to provide an effective solution then you need to make sure the cost of invention or acquisition are in the financial models and it could well impact your discount factor (project ßeta).

Do you have, across all functions:

- The right people?
- Enough capital?
- Enough cash?
- The right sales force?
- The right knowledge?
- The right management control system?
- The right distribution model?
- Access to the right KOL's?
- The right vendor base?
- Enough mfg. capacity?
- The proper internal systems? Etc.

For any sub-point no, you may plan to acquire the missing aspect that lead to a no; just make sure you discount the probability of success and account for its cost.

When you bring it all together, the high-level scoring is simple: if you don't have yes, yes, yes, then move on. If you have some narrowly classified noes, you may want to move to a higher level of accuracy. Just remember that the goal is to eliminate the losers and select the winners. Make a decision and move on.

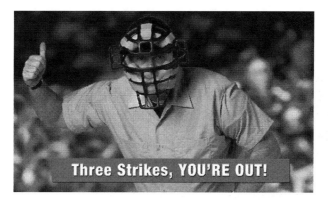

Three Strikes, YOU'RE OUT!

LESSONS

1. When comparing opportunities it is critical that you have standards for all variables

2. External input to the opportunity assessment is critical

3. Beware of political favorites

LESSON 23
STATE THE OPPORTUNITY SIZE WITH INTEGRITY

THE STORY

I recently completed teaching a Marketing Management course at the MBA level. In the same time frame, I was working with a start-up medical device company advising on their investor deck. I reached a common realization. There is a natural tendency to inflate market projections by capturing every conceivable dollar potential worldwide. There is nothing unethical or morally wrong in putting your absolute best foot forward. But there is no value in inflating the opportunity.

My professional opinion is that the revenue or potential opportunity you quote must be congruent with your overall story and plan. Angels, VCs and VPs of Marketing are too savvy to be drawn into an overstated market potential.

It is better to progress the story through the fair market potential to the realizable potential, quickly and then tell your story (plan) and state the five-year revenue forecast, then dwelling on a fantasy.

If your story doesn't sound like it is worth it, or, if it doesn't deliver on the expectations of Sr. Management don't fudge the model, change the story.

OVER THE TOP MARKET ASSESSMENT

By over-the-top I am referring to the fact that every marketing plan I see states that the product represents a billion-dollar opportunity. Not every marketing plan has a chance at reaching a billion dollars, and that is OK. If it does, it might be well beyond the timeline for a needed return.

REALIZABLE MARKET OPPORTUNITY

In general, there are exclusions from the Grand market that are driven by the nature of your product. If the product has a narrow indication or is a line extension, it probably is not worth a billion dollars, ever. It may be the first of five applications needed to reach full potential. It is not productive to spend a disproportional amount of time explaining the grand potential, mention it and move on to your story. As much as you would like to think that the most important thing to the reader is the huge market opportunity, it is not.

Most humans are risk adverse. They would rather see a tight story as to how you will realize the revenue forecast than create a dreamscape for the future.

TARGETED MARKET OPPORTUNITY

I read with delight as a student defined the nature of the customer segment that they believed they would be successful with or in. By having a customer target, which you should have, you exclude a section of the Realizable Market Potential. If your segment represents only a quarter of the realizable potential, then reduce that number by 25%.

REVENUE FORECAST

Once you know the Target Market Potential, you continue to discount your potential for factors such as:

- ◆ Competition
- ◆ Capacity
- ◆ Market attractiveness (Did the product end up with the features and benefits you had hoped for?)
- ◆ Channel leverage
- ◆ The number of outlets
- ◆ The number of direct sales representatives
- ◆ Access to the targeted customers
- ◆ Launch timing
- ◆ Environmental barriers

Last but not least, you need to have a beta factor (ß) a final reduction in your target market that represents the unknown and the unknowable. How do you calculate this last discount factor? You look to history either internal or external to your company. How accurate have your prediction been in the past. Do you have positive or negative reasons to believe that you will be as accurate this time?

Typically, the revenue forecasts are seldom realized. Of the 100+ products I have launched, more of them under perform in the first year than over perform. After 30 years of product forecasting you would think that I could get the first-year launch numbers correct. But there is always the unknowable and the X factor. The X factor is the political (not always bad) aspects of revenue forecasts. Typically, there is what you believe and then what everyone else is willing to bet on. Plot your actual performance against both numbers and learn.

Remember that your marketing plan moves through the project with you. At each step, you need to add credibility by validating any and all assumption you have baked into the story. (E.g. the first version assumed that R&D would delivery on the utility that you wanted to commercialize. Some subsequent revision accounts for whether they did or did not).

The challenge to increasing accuracy with time is keeping the caveats and assumptions clearly in the mind of top management as decisions are made. I have been in many discussions just before launch where a Sr. manager reminded me that my original forecast numbers where much larger than they are now at launch. You need to be prepared to answer that challenge without throwing the manager or the team under the bus.

LESSONS

1. Have complete transparency for every reason you discount the opportunity
2. Have complete transparency for every source you use
3. Always assume the positive

PRICING A NEW MEDICAL DEVICE

THE STORY

A prospective client approached me recently, who needed help in setting the price for the new medical device they were about to commercialize. We sat down to go over the project and they indeed needed help. The first thing he told me was that they needed a 65% margin and the fully burdened manufacturing cost of the device was expected to be $50.00, the plan was to price the device at $150.00.

I said great! You have met your goals. He stared at me for a while and then said, "but I think it is worth a lot more than $150.00." As he got up and started to leave I said, "Why do you think it is worth more than $150.00?" He responded, "if they use my device instead of how they do it today, they can save time, reduce nursing injuries, and reduce their stocking inventories".

The prospective client had put the cart before the horse, and instinctively knew it.

Understanding the value proposition of the device (the devices utility), in the eyes of the clinician users and economic buyers, is the first step. Pricing is the monetizing of that value, the second step.

PRICING STRATEGY

I am a big fan of writing out your pricing strategy very early in the commercialization process. Start with your financial goals, your unit / time goals, your situational analysis and the value proposition. Craft a sentence that best describes your intentions with respect to pricing.

We set our price to ensure that we signal a congruent message with our value proposition, garner at least 50% of the added value of our widget, we are profitable and we are 80% confident that the price does not become a barrier to success in more than 20% of the A accounts.

PRICING

The art of monetizing value, pricing, is just that an art. I have spent as much as $140,000 doing value + pricing studies. I've spent as little as nothing. You need to do a situational review before you set off on value or price determination. By understanding the situation, you can "right size" your effort (risk stratify the work). This is especially important for start-ups who need efficiency over effectiveness.

With setting price, it is never one size fits all. Here is a partial list of the questions that will lead you to understanding your pricing situation better:

1. What is the nature of the product that you are launching?

   a. Commodity
   b. Line extension
   c. Line expansion
   d. New product area within your current portfolio
   e. New portfolio
   f. Disruptive technology

2. What is the nature of the market into which you are launching the product?

   a. Current geography or new geography
   b. New segment or current segment
   c. New customer base or current base
   d. New channel or current channel
   e. Will there be value added services or not

3. Determine the risk if you under or over value the product?

   a. How forgiving have your customers been historically
   b. Do they give you second bites at the apple
   c. What are the consequences if you price incorrectly out of the gate?
      i. Do you slow the momentum down
      ii. Do you cast doubt in the minds of the customers about the value of the product
   d. What will the competitive response be to a pricing error?

WATCH OUT!

It is critical that your value proposition and your price point support each other. If you are talking about the device as, the greatest advancement of the therapy and you price it at the same price point of old technology, it sets up a disconnect in the hearts and minds of the target customer. You have to resolve that disconnect before they emotionally accept the value story.

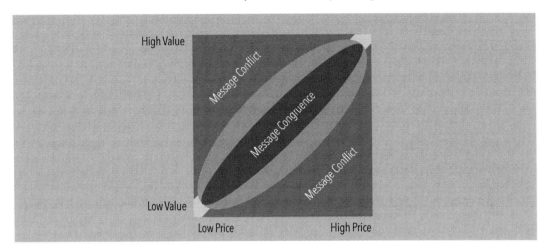

SO HOW DO I SET A PRICE?
I am not trying to be disingenuous, but it depends. As a general rule of thumb, I try to split the increased value with the customer. For example, if my perspective client demonstrated an increase in hard value of 30% over the current state of the art product, I would increase my price, volume for volume, by 30% over the competition, hoping to realize 15%.

CAVEATS
In the medical device space, there are always nuances that need to be considered. Reimbursement and service line profitability are always two potential barriers to realizing the true value of a new product. If the hospital service can absorb the premium and there are savings within that service, then you may get the full value of the device. However, when you are selling into a service line that is barely profitable and you are changing their reimbursement/cost relationship, you may not get all you had hoped for.

A HAPPY ENDING
We did the work to determine the added utility that the product in question brought to the critical care nurses and it came out to a 100% increase over the current technique. Total cost for the current technique was monetized at $308.00. Some of that 100% was based on a reduction of inventory cost, some was on saving time and some was on increased safety for the nurses (a reduction in lost time accidents). Our hypothesized price point was $600, not the $150 that the client had targeted.

We tested the monetization with a few nurse managers and no matter how much evidence we showed them, they just could not get their minds and hearts to accept the $600 value. Strategically, if we had priced the device at the point that we could justify, we would have either slowed acceptance, lowered demand, or failed all together.

Because the risk of being wrong had both a high probability (based on the initial qualitative interviews) and a high severity (given the financial state of the company) additional testing was warranted. We surveyed 30 key customers in the US. We selected the Van Westendorp technique as our methodology. We discovered that 65% of our 30 surveyed customers would consider the product a good value between $300 - $400 dollars. An additional 23% indicated that they would consider $400 - $500 too expensive for general use, but would still purchase the device. Historically, I would have set the price point in the $450.00 range. There is typically a low bias when using survey methods to determine price points. However, in this case we set the Average Selling Price at $375.00 and held firm to that target. List price was set at $400.00.

We exceeded the target profit margin, we garnered a premium over current technology, and we did not inhibit the sales process. A win-win-win result!

LESSONS

1. Pricing is an art, so take the science with a grain of salt
2. Always error on the high side for list price
3. Pricing should be the last topic in any discussion with a customer

---

LESSON 25

BE THE VISION KEEPER FOR
MEDICAL DEVICE PRODUCT DEVELOPMENT

THE STORY

A great product manager friend of mine had spent three (3) years driving a product to market. At long last he was on the precipice of launch and his wife read the value proposition and said to him, "I don't buy it." Normally, this off- handed comment would not have affected him. However, in this case his wife was also a prospective customer. He started to doubt the product concept and reached out to me as a second set of eyes.

This product should have taken 18 months to get ready for launch. However, several personnel issues, technical challenges and a poor shifting regulatory strategy had made the commercialization process a huge battle. He had invested so much emotional energy in just getting it ready for launch that he had lost the vision.

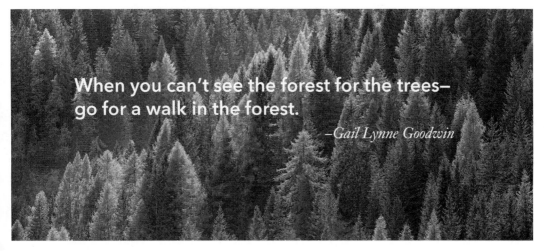

When you can't see the forest for the trees—
go for a walk in the forest.

—*Gail Lynne Goodwin*

As you roll the Value Proposition through the R&D phases toward commercialization, it is easy to get lost in the day-to-day effort it takes. But from time to time, you need to stop and separate yourself from the emotional connection you have to your device and ask, "Is this product still relevant? Is it still believable?" (Or have a trusted colleague do it for you). He became so busy helping the team be successful that he had compromised his commitment to constantly check in with the customer along the way to see if he was still on course.

THE VISION IS JOB 1
Once you propose a product concept and get the ball rolling within your

company, you need to, as best you can free yourself of the inevitable details of product management and stay in a pure marketing mindset. You are the only one who can be the keeper of the Vision. Your role is to sell the vision, over and over and over again. Keep the team on course. Don't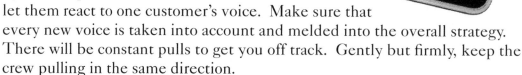
let them react to one customer's voice. Make sure that every new voice is taken into account and melded into the overall strategy. There will be constant pulls to get you off track. Gently but firmly, keep the crew pulling in the same direction.

Utilize your customers to help. Periodic check-ins to see how you are progressing toward that destination is critical.

WHAT IF WE DO GET OFF TRACK?

The worst thing is to launch a product and have it flop. Launches cost $100,000 to millions of dollars. The opportunity cost for the sales organization is huge. Not least is the hit your department's reputation takes for future launches. If you keep checking the Vision's viability and if the product is living up to that Vision, you should be OK. But if something is off, raise the flag! If you raise the flag early enough, course correction might be at a team level only. Raise the flag too late in the process and then it will be out of the teams' hands. Either way you need to raise the flag. In an intelligent organization, the raising of a flag is not the career limiting action you might fear. Not raising the flag and flopping might well be career ending.

WHAT TYPE OF THINGS CAN GET YOU OFF COURSE?

Unfortunately, a whole lot of things can blow you off course. Both internal and external aspect of the opportunity can change. Some of the things to be aware of are:

- Technical design decisions that seem benign to engineers can really sneak up on you and do damage to the value proposition.
- Competition can beat you to launch with a similar product
- A new technique or substitute technology can blow you out of the water
- The cost of the product may preclude you from being profitable, the temptation will be to raise your target price until you are profitable, and however, you may price yourself right out of the market.
- The incidence and prevalence of the problem you were solving may change.
- There may have been an untested assumption that raised it's head later in the process and proved more impactful than originally thought.

and there are many, many, more.

   This is why you need to continue to validate your original beliefs. Keep the environmental scan sweeping the skies around your product Vision. Take a lesson from the military and don't shut down the radar after the first sweep. Things change with time and events.

HOW DID THE STORY END?
My friend was OK. His wife's hospital was not in his customer segment. He stopped the full launch and did a soft launch into only targeted centers and everything went well. Not perfect. Some of the decisions that were made at the team level with respect to design were changed to optimize acceptance within the target. The changes did not trigger a new regulatory filing and delayed the launch by 3 months.
   In the defined segment the product is now number one in unit share! The segment did turn out to be smaller than expected.

LESSONS
1. Create the vision
2. Share the vision often
3. Live the vision

LESSON 26
NEW PRODUCT LAUNCH PLANNING TOPICS FOR THE MEDICAL DEVICE MARKET

THE SET UP

Over the years, I have been privileged to launch or direct the launch of near-ly 100 medical devices. With that experience I have learned that launching a new product is not a marketing function. It takes an integrated team with an integrated mindset. I have assisted a number of clients in designing their new product launch plans. Several long-time colleagues have recently asked me to provide a thought check-list for their less experienced team members to aid in launch planning.

I have decided to share that check list with everyone. I caution that this is a list of decisions or thinking that should occur as you are designing your launch. Following this check list doesn't guarantee success. So much of the success comes from the quality and depth of thinking you put into the topics. With that cautionary note, here is the check list. A conceptual thought that might make this clear to you is to think about the topics as section titles slide for the Launch deck.

THE INTENT WITH AN INTEGRATED LAUNCH

The way I have always thought about a product launch is parallel to a rocket launch. Planned well (correct trajectory to achieve the proper orbit) you ap-ply a tremendous amount energy (time, resources, targeting) to a launch and once you break free of Earth's gravity (market resistance to change) you fly along at a speed of 17,500 miles per hour with no fuel being utilized at all.

THE THOUGHT CHECK-LIST

Launch Summary

- ❏ Product vision
- ❏ Elevator pitch regarding the launch, not the product

Market Understanding

- ❏ Therapy understanding
- ❏ Technology understanding
- ❏ Macro segmentation
- ❏ Competition defined
- ❏ Market drivers determined
- ❏ Key success factors identified

Product Understanding

- ❏ Product definition
- ❏ Product description
- ❏ Positioning statement
- ❏ Value proposition
- ❏ Health economic story
- ❏ FAQ
- ❏ Trouble shooting guide
- ❏ Allowed claims
- ❏ Competitive comparison
- ❏ Portfolio relevance

Launch Strategy

Launch goals/objectives

Financial

- ❏ Revenue
- ❏ Profit
- ❏ Share shifting rate

Non-Financial

- ❏ Quality
- ❏ Complaint
- ❏ Success rate
- ❏ Compliance to targeting

- ❐ Business process metrics
- ❐ VOC
- ❐ Customer satisfaction product
- ❐ Customer satisfaction service
- ❐ Customer targeting
- ❐ Channel considerations
- ❐ Customer profile
- ❐ Customer engagement strategy
- ❐ External communication strategy

Launch Tactics

- ❐ Launch structure (Controlled, Limited, General)
- ❐ Launch campaign development
- ❐ Team membership
- ❐ Launch calendar
- ❐ Sales process (Controlled, Limited, General)
- ❐ Product sampling plan
- ❐ Evaluation process steps identified and facilitated
- ❐ Pricing (Controlled, Limited, General)
- ❐ Reimbursement
- ❐ Demand generation plan
- ❐ Sales pipeline projections (1-12 months)
- ❐ Demand/Supply plan
- ❐ Revenue projections
- ❐ Share penetration rates
- ❐ Service plan
- ❐ Sales training progession plan

Messaging Mix Development

- ❐ Message development
- ❐ Collateral development plan
- ❐ Video
- ❐ In-service video
- ❐ Promotional video
- ❐ Testimonial video
- ❐ Digital
- ❐ Print

- ❑ Promotion
- ❑ Trade Show plan / calendar / collateral
- ❑ Poster and Podium plan
- ❑ Advertising plan / calendar / collateral
- ❑ PR plan / collateral
- ❑ Social Media Use plan

LAUNCH CONTROLS

- ❑ Team dashboard
- ❑ Management dashboard
- ❑ Quality dashboard
- ❑ Sales detail dashboard

PRODUCT CLAIMS

- ❑ Current claims
- ❑ Desired claims
- ❑ Gap analysis
- ❑ Clinical evidence collection plan
- ❑ Regulatory strategy

MULTI-GENERATIONAL PRODUCT PORTFOLIO PLAN

LAUNCH BUDGET / SPENDING PLAN BY QUARTER OVER 12 MONTHS

LESSONS

1. Sharing the thinking behind the plan is often times more valuable than the written plan

2. Not every launch will require all the check boxes to be checked. However, I strongly recommend that you think through the inclusion and exclusion of content from the list, defend the "in" and "out" decisions

3. The higher the complexity of the technology / product / launch process the more likely it will be that you need to address each and every thought

LESSON 27
WRITING A GREAT NEW PRODUCT LAUNCH OBJECTIVE FOR THE MEDICAL DEVICE MARKET

THE SET UP

All Marketing Strategy development must start with a clearly stated objective. Preferably one that links directly to the Corporate strategic plan. The richer the objective is, then the more right on target the strategy will be.

What is a typical, but poorly thought out Marketing Objective?

- Dominate the xyz segment.
- Destroy the competition.
- Go to number one in unit share for the xyz product class
- Reach $100,000,000 in sales by January 20xx.
- Enter the XYZ product segment in North America, while achieving a 76% GM on all sales.
- Must be successful in 200 accounts by Christmas (Which Christmas and what is successful?)

You may have received marching orders like these before. Why are they not actionable?

They don't provide any insight into why, how, or how not to accomplish the goal or objective. They are all too general. It is a delicate balance between being prescriptive and too general.

At the very least make your objective(s) or goal(s) a SMART one.

S – Specific

M – Measurable

A – Achievable

R – Resource limits

T – Time bound

Your SMART goal(s) should include some of the follow characteristics of a launch:

◆ Quality

◆ Timing

◆ Cost

◆ Adherence to plan

◆ Share (dollars or units)

◆ Penetration rate

◆ Repeat orders

◆ Customer satisfaction levels

Make all definitions as specific as possible.

WHAT DOES A GREAT MARKETING OBJECTIVE LOOK LIKE?

The objective for the launch of our newest widget is to be the first to enter the growing North America segment of xxxx therapy, to grow revenue in the over all xyz business and provide a full product line. Hence, blocking any in roads ZZZ competitor might make with their widget expected to launch 6 months after our widget.

Goal Metrics

◆ Penetrate 22 targeted Pioneering and Early Adopter accounts within 3-months post launch.

◆ Establish an overall successful close rate of 85%.

◆ Achieve a 95% re-order rate for every account closed within the first 9-months post launch.

◆ Average cost to close a targeted account should not exceed $1,000.

◆ Realize $25 million in new sales within the first 12-months post launch.

◆ Cannibalize no more 10% of the existing Xwidet and Zwidet sales.

◆ Every representative or agent engaged must close 2 accounts within 6-months post launch.

- Clinical/technical success will match the clinical/technical success rate of the pivotal trial results as reported at XXX conference.
- On time delivery of product 98% orders in by 3PM EST shipped by 5PM EST same day.
- 100% of product complaints are filed within 12 hours of first notification and are investigated within the second 12 hours.
- Product return rate will not exceed 2% of units shipped within the first 6-months post launch.

INTERNAL VALIDATION OF INTEGRATED GOALS IS CRITICAL

If you develop a weekly dashboard you can monitor the progress toward each of these goals and act accordingly. But please internally validate the legitimacy of the goals. As an example, could 22 accounts produce $25 M in revenue? Did your soft launch suggest that you could achieve an 85% close rate? Is there enough accounts that you can win in 22 of them and not cannibalize more than 10% of the other product sales?

If you spend a week developing the right goals to match with your objectives it is more than worth it.

Once you have the objective the way you want it and it is approved by Sr. management, then you can design your strategy to meet the critical aspects of the objective and your tactical plan will have met all the criteria that you need.

"The way to achieve our goals is to hold them tightly and our strategies [tactics] loosely."   —*Megan Hyatt Miller*

LESSONS

1. Always start with goals or objectives before strategy
2. Only as complicated as need be
3. Make sure the objectives are in support of company imperatives

COMMERCIALIZATION
IDEA GENERATION
BRAND
IMPROVEMENT
SUCCESS
MANUFACTURE
IMPROVE
product
ANALYTICS
PROCESS
ANALYSIS
STAGE
ANALYTICS
BRAND
DEVELOPMENT
DESIGN
NEW
PRODUCT
DEVELOPMENT
DEVELOPMENT
IMPROVE
MANAGEMENT
IMPLEMENTATION
IDEA
BUSINESS
STAGE
ANALYSIS
IDEA GENERATION
process
IMPROVE
MARKETING
BUSINESS
COMMERCIALIZATION
PLAN
implementation
analytics
DESIGN
manufacture
MANAGEMENT
MARKETING
PRICING
STRATEGY

Marketing's Role in Product Development

As a medical device marketer, your role with respect to R&D is to provide a Vision for the outcome of any new product development project that is started in your product area. By providing a link to the customer and the customer's environment in which the R&D team can derive a context for your new product vision, whether that be in person or through story telling.

Always reach for the Stars with your Vision, if you fall short you land on the moon - still an out of this world success.

There is always a natural tension between all functional departments. If you can get the Vision right and owned by the Development team the natural and necessary tensions and competing agendas will fall subordinate to the grander Vision.

Judiciously utilize the clinical customer as a lever to redirect wandering development team members. Managing the interaction and relationships among the different team members will be a source of frustration if you lose your Vision. Make the journey as fun as possible.

It never ceases to amaze me how the tiniest design decisions can sink a promising R&D process. As the keeper of the vision stay involved on as detailed level as you can. Be as detailed as possible with product requirements and stay focused on the outcomes, not the how's.

LESSON 28

HIGH LEVEL PRODUCT REQUIREMENT CREATION FOR NEW MEDICAL DEVICES

THE SET UP

So once again the goal is to provide an awareness of the process and provide a couple of tips regarding "How To".

If you gain nothing more than one "aha" out of this lesson then it was well worth reading.

There are three or four approaches to requirements planning. All of them can work. The process I layout for you here is a straight forward practical approach.

The big caution is reflected in the adjacent cartoon. To avoid the miscommunication take your time creating the Vision statement, Business problem statement, Clinician problem statement and ultimately the initial Product positioning and Value proposition statements.

How the customer explained it

What the customer really needed

How the junior marketer described it

How the project leader understood it

What was launched

THE HIGH LEVEL PROCESS

Recognize a new product opportunity from the portfolio planning process we have identified that we are vulnerable to collateral share loss in one specific area of our portfolio. Our market scan produced the realization that we don't have a product in a fast growth segment of the market, perhaps more importantly three of our key competitors do.

WRITE DOWN THE BUSINESS PROBLEM STATEMENT(S)

Write the problem statement(s) using general language. Note that you may have two or more problem statements. That's cool. You could write it as a business problem, a portfolio problem, and /or a risk problem. A good start. Eventually you need to write it as a customer problem. Capturing the unresolved issues that the fast growing segment is resolving.

CONDUCT A QUALITATIVE MARKET SCAN

Before you write the solution hypothesis you need to gather additional input from the market. At this point in the process I would urge you to collect structured well documented qualitative data; don't skip forward to conducting statistically valid market research just yet. I have spent as little as $25,000 and as much as $1.4 million on market research to determine a winning product definition. It is too big of a financial investment to dive right in without a little background work first.

Now is the time for a little sleuthing, search the MAUDE data base for complaint histories on all three competitive products. Categorize the complaints by type. I typically will capture the categorized data in an Excel table. Obtain product specification for each of the three products (sale literature, IFUs from the website, 510k applications, general web search). Next, interview a couple of your top territory managers who have reported competitive activity in their hospitals. Have your sales force poll their accounts to determine who is using these new products. Identify which of your friendly accounts have committed to purchasing the new product (try to interview at least one representative account for each of the three competitive products). Arrange personal one-on-one interviews with each of these committed friendly accounts. The typical product marketing questons should suffice at this point:

- What is/are the challenge(s) you are/were trying to overcome by using this new product?
- How did you try to meet these challenges before you had the new device?
- Why do you believe that this type of product will meet your needs?
- What do you like about the product?
- What don't you like about the product?
- What type of proof and metrics would you need to see to believe that the product will meet your needs?
- What are important features or attributes of this type of product? (try to get this input prioritized, at least ranked and rated)
- If there was one aspect of the product you could improve what would it be?

WRITE THE CLINICAL PROBLEM STATEMENT AS YOU UNDERSTAND IT AFTER THE DISCOVERY PROCESS

At this stage the problem statement can be several pages long. In general, the contents of a good problem statement should include:

- A re-statement of the original problem statement that the competitive products were design for,

- The residual unmet needs for each of the three product solutions (gap assessment)
- A summary of the MAUDE database review
- A summary of claims made in the regulatory filings
- A summary of warnings and cautions from the IFUs
- A summary of the clinical trial data if any were required
- A summary of any editorials or press announcements regarding the products
- Competitive metrics: share, growth rate, revenue, ASP, archetypal description of customers

CAUTION: Don't become so focused on the gaps or potential solutions for the gaps that you forget to use fresh eyes on the original problem.

The discovery process that has been described can be done in as little as a couple of weeks or it could take a few months. The creativity comes from you as to how you do the work economically or efficiently. Just don't skip this step.

Now you have enough information to define the problem. This will be the vision statement for your R&D team as well as management.

QUANTITATIVE MARKET RESEARCH

Hopefully, your vision statement / problem statement has been compelling enough to warrant a further investment by senior management to execute a formal VOC process that will include additional qualitative and your initial quantitative research.

For now let's focus on the output. For me the most effective way to look at the output of the initial quantitative research is in a stacked spider /radar chart. A spider/radar chart produces a geometric picture of the shape of possible solution sets for the unmet needs.

DESCRIPTION OF A RADAR/SPIDER CHART

Each of the axis of a radar chart represents a benefit/feature/attribute of the solution set. These are the most critical aspects of the product to the customer. The scores are a reflection of how well the product meets their needs. The scale is arbitrary, I typically will use 0-10. The end product in this scenario would have five (5) separate geometric plots.

1. The ideal or perfect scores for the general market
2. The ideal or perfect set of scores for your chosen segment
3. Competitor 1 scores
4. Competitor 2 scores
5. Competitor 3 scores

In the example provided you can see that the two series of data have markedly different shapes. The ideal solution for this general population would be the connecting of all the highest scores of each axis. This would provide you with a third geometric shape. By looking at the differences between the first two series and the newly created third one you get a feeling for the gaps. You can plainly see that the red series has a biased solution that delivers on the left axis and the blue to the right. Knowing this and combining it with the balance of what you learned from your competitive analysis you can determine what your new product strategy could be. There will be several biases that you can select from.

The big watch out here is to use the qualitative research to make sure your axis are the critical ones for success of your new solution. Your ultimate success with this new product will be directly linked to how well you determine the critical success factors or axis to plot.

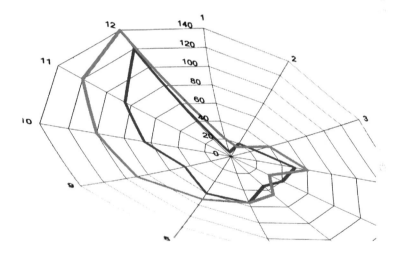

LESSONS

1. Avoid technical language, focus on clinical language

2. Let the customer guide the input as well as provide the input

3. Don't worry about how R&D will meet the requirements at this point

VOC INPUT FOR PRODUCT REQUIREMENTS DEVELOPMENT

THE SET UP

Regardless of how you package or communicate the Product Requirements for a new product there must be a customer input process that precedes finalizing of those requirements. Collecting the Voice Of Customer (VOC) is critical to the success of new product creation.

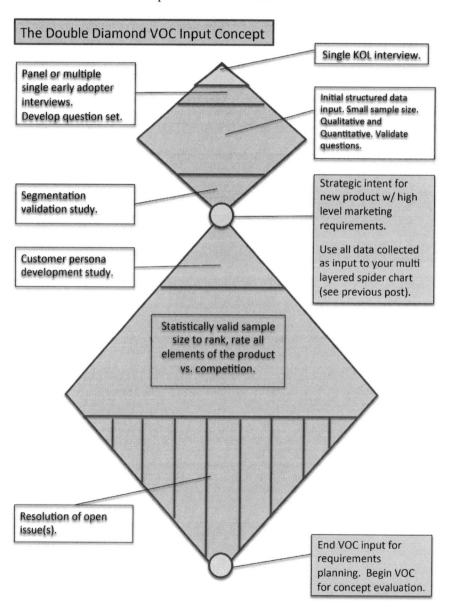

The Double Diamond VOC Input Concept

Single KOL interview.

Panel or multiple single early adopter interviews.
Develop question set.

Initial structured data input. Small sample size. Qualitative and Quantitative. Validate questions.

Segmentation validation study.

Strategic intent for new product w/ high level marketing requirements.

Customer persona development study.

Use all data collected as input to your multi layered spider chart (see previous post).

Statistically valid sample size to rank, rate all elements of the product vs. competition.

Resolution of open issue(s).

End VOC input for requirements planning. Begin VOC for concept evaluation.

THE DOUBLE DIAMOND PROCESS™

Sometimes a picture is worth 10,000 words. The chart shown to the left is the way I explain the approach to building that VOC into a fully validated set of requirements.

The key in the progression of confidence as you move down the double diamond. As you move through each section you gain the understanding and confidence in the data to which you need to draw your insight from.

CAUTION

If you want to assure the greatest chance of success don't skip a step or stop early.

LESSONS

1. Start simple
2. Risk adjust the sample size
3. You are never "done" with VOC

LESSON 30

MINIMUM VIABLE PRODUCTS (MVP) IN THE MEDICAL DEVICE MARKET

THE SET UP

I recently attended the VIVA2016 conference held in Las Vegas. I ran into a number of marketing wizards there. Several of them challenged my perceived opposition to using the MVP product strategy for medical devices.

CLARIFICATION

Let me be clear, I am not opposed to the use of the MVP concept. It can be very valauble. My concern is in how it is used by those who are not well schooled in the device world. I have found with many inventor / entrepreneurs (brilliant people all of them) that they latch on to these concepts at a superficial level and could be setting themselves up for failure or worst yet, hurting people.

WHAT IS MEANT BY MVP?

When Eric Ries used the term for the first time he defined it this way: "A Minimum Viable Product is that version of a new product which allows a team to collect the maximum amount of validated learning about customers with the least effort." Nowhere in this definition does he mention commercial viability. For the device world, this may well be represented by a clinical trial.

THE CAUTION?
We have to be careful when extending management (marketing) concepts across markets and industries. While there is a huge opportunity to learn from concepts formulated in other markets, sectors, industries and disciplines we can't assume that they can be directly applied. We have to be good Marketers and review all the assumptions and environmental consideration and then apply them in our context.

We have seen where the application of Software or App development thinking has failed in the medical device space. How one manages the risk of failure is very different when the result is death or serious injury vs. being disappointed. Minecraft, the now very popular digital game was launched commercially after only 6 weeks of development and was barely functional. It was however a great application of MVP. It served as a proof of concept. It offered a complete game, just not a very finished one. The risk of failure in Minecraft did not include death or serious injury to a real human.

One example (not a perfect one) of this is Theranos. They produced an MVP that failed to offer complete clinical utility (clearly an over simplification, but illustrative none-the-less). We will leave the why to others. Great concept, great story, great funding but the product just didn't offer a complete clinical solution to the problem.

But a great quote from the reporter that broke the story that appeared in Vanity Fair's article on Theranos, ...Carreyrou was simply emboldened. "It's OK if you've got a smartphone app or a social network, and you go live with it before it's ready; people aren't going to die," ... "But with medicine, it's different."

THE CONCEPT
In Medical Device Development (MDD), the V in MVP is huge and unyielding. In today's world the term Viable is getting bigger. It could be expressed as:

$$V = f(S+R+CCU+C+\$)$$

V = viable

S = safe

R = regulatory cleared or approved

CCU = offers a complete clinical solution

C = the promise of Cost neutrality

$ = a pathway to reimbursement

What do I mean when I say "complete clinical utility (CCU)." Once you get to the clinic you need to offer "complete clinical utility". You must completely (minimally) solve the clinical problem that you were attacking. If you don't you have delivered no real value to the clinician. By all means leave the sprinkles and glaze off, but give them a whole doughnut.

What I do find helpful is the idea of "fast to failure" referring to prototyping, at all three levels: concept, feasibility, and design. These prototypes can be partial, abstract, bread boards through Verification testing samples, but they don't get near a patient.

(Minimum viable product)   (Product)

A DIFFERENT WAY TO THINK ABOUT MVP

Fully integrated multi-generational product planning. A documented, data driven, customer focused pathway to delivering 100% customer satisfaction in steps. This type of plan can span decades as with the Left Ventricular Assist Devices (LVAD). Or, it can take just a few years as with the SMART Stent.

Multi-Generational Product Map

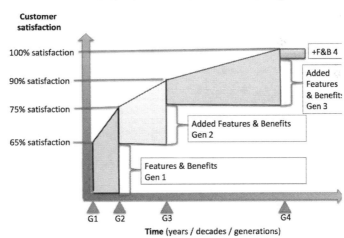

Call it what you will, MVP, CCU, multi-generational planning, doesn't matter. Whatever you do, make it safe.

LESSONS

1. Must completely solve the clinical problem
2. Planned benefit expansion is better than guessing or being reactive
3. Viable is a really big concept in the medical device space

MARKET RISK IDENTIFICATION IN PRODUCT PORTFOLIO PLANNING FOR THE MEDICAL DEVICE MARKET

THE SET UP
Recently I mentioned using a Monte Carlo approach to determining market risk that you should address with your Product Portfolio Plan (PPP). I thought I would take a minute to describe the approach. As a reminder this lesson deals with only one of three key dimensions of settting your goals for your Portfolio Plan. The PPP should maximize the impact that your new product investment has on your companies performance in the Market.

I developed a tool as a way of garnering agreement with Sr. management that we were trying to solve the right problem with our Portfolio Planning Process. So when we started the Portfolio Planning process we had a revenue target, a resource allocation budget and a risk profile projected forward over the 5-8 year period of the Portfolio Plan. The three dimensional aspects of budget, revenue goals and risk profile will help focus your Product Portfolio Plan on the right targets. Without clear targets you can't optimize the plan. Don't underestimate the challenge of garnering agreement on the targets.

Einstein indicated that if he were given an hour to solve a problem he would spend the first 55 minutes making sure he understood the question.

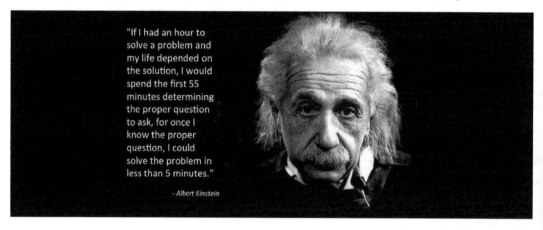

"If I had an hour to solve a problem and my life depended on the solution, I would spend the first 55 minutes determining the proper question to ask, for once I know the proper question, I could solve the problem in less than 5 minutes."

- Albert Einstein

The tool is the application of the FMEA methodology into a Monte Carlo method for determining the current assessment of risk in your market, or product segment.

WHAT IS A MONTE CARLO APPROACH?
In general, a Monte Carlo approach is used when you have insufficient data to make a definitive decision. But you need to get started, so you are better off

polling the true experts in a field and after their consideration of the issue or problem you accept their concensus recommendation or finding as fact. Validate and adjust your actions from that starting point. Long-term experience suggests that you will be 80% correct, at least this is how I think about it.

A Monte Carlo method is not taking a wild guess with three of your buddies. The preferred approach would be to spend a bunch of money, do a ton of research and take several years to figure out your portfolio plan. For companies that are resource constrained or time restricted a Monte Carlo approach, as described here, is a great first step.

When applying a Monte Carlo approach in determining market risk I have adopted the Failure Modes and Effects Analysis (FMEA) methodology that is used through out the industry in product design. Using a specific and well understood method will help in documenting the process and the findings.

So when applying this to determine the consensus beliefs about market risks you follow the steps below:

CONDUCTING THE MODIFIED FMEA PROCESS

Step 1 Identify industry experts (internal and external to your company)

Step 2 Have them write down the issues that give them pause, cause worry or keep them up late at night, etc.

Step 3 Compile the issues lists and combine where duplicates appear. If you get over a dozen you might want to think about re-writing them to combine a few into a broader category.

Step 4 Create a table that have the Issues listed, any description for clarification purposes and two blank columns titled Impact and Probability of occurrence.

Step 5 Assign a 1-5 scale for Impact and a 1-5 scale for Probability of occurrence. These scale definitions are critical and a bit tricky to develop.

> Issues should be as specific as possible. An example of an issue might be: Competitor X will launch their version of our new product Z, X number of months before we do.

Step 6 Have the same panel of experts score the issues with the two scales. Each issue is scored 1-5 for impact and 1-5 for probability.

Step 7 Compile the results. Distributions and means. With the issues that have bi-modal distributions you need to go back and have a discussion to ensure that the issues were well defined.

Step 8 Once you have one pair of numbers, impact and probability it is time to plot them on a chart that has impact on the y-axis and the probability of the x axis. Let say that you had 11 major issues identified by your panel of experts. The 11 issues would be plotted as shown below. Note this is an illustration only.

		PROBABILITY OF OCCURRENCE				
Red / Yellow / Green		5	4	3	2	1
	5	1, 4, 8				
	4		2, 9		3, 11	
SEVERITY IF OCCURRED	3			5, 6		
	2		7	10		
	1					

So to read this chart one would say, issue number 1 has an impact of 5 and a probability of 5 so the total risk is 25 points. Practically, depending on how you have defined the scales, this would be a catastrophic impact and a near certainty that it would happen, clearly a situation that needs resolving before completing the planning process.

Step 9 This chart will give you your market risk profile. Anything clearly in the red needs to be addressed by some aspect of the Strategic plan and if appropriate the Product Portfolio Plan.

Step 10 Reflect each issue that is in the red, back into the portfolio planning process. This will produce a mitigation plan.

Step 11 Have your expert panel rescore the issues taking into account the mitigations (how you changed the plan or added to it). Plot the new scores. You now have a before and after market risk profile.

Step 12 Once you are satisfied with the new profile, rank the impact that each product program produced. You may have 5-12 product programs that are required to mitigate the risks. Each program could impact multiple risk factors. These impacts should be additive in your prioritization scoring.

		PROBABILITY OF OCCURRENCE				
Red / Yellow / Green		5	4	3	2	1
SEVERITY IF OCCURRED	5					
	4				3, 11	2, 9
	3		4, 8	5, 6		
	2	1	7	10		
	1					

EXAMPLE: Let's say the issue is an emerging trend toward minimally invasive surgery (MIS) [issue number 2] and you had no products in the pipeline that addressed this emerging trend, currently rated a 4,4 risk score. You added a new product development project to the plan that moved [2] to a 4,1 risk score, you have reduced the aggregate risk of this issue by 12 (16-4) a reduction in risk by 12 points. Let say that issue 9 was a lack of product innovation with respect to market leadership. The vision for the MIS project also helped reduce that risk issue as well, moving [9] producing a risk reduction of 12 points. When ranking the product dev projects the MIS project would receive 24 risk reduction points.

This ranking will provide one of the three key elements of prioritizing the Portfolio for funding. In the end you will use three ranking scales to rank your investment.

When the portfolio plan is completed you need to make sure you have updated the Market risk profile to reflect the final map based on what was ultimately funded.

Seem complicated? It is at first, once you have done it then you will see the simplicity and logic in it. That is why you must be disciplined in this approach.

CAUTION: The first time you use this approach do not try to do it alone. There are multiple tricky aspects that might lead you down the wrong road. Call me for one on one coaching or to sign me up to consult you through it.

LESSONS

1. Risk and impact definition are critical
2. Get help the first time
3. Constantly review this risk assessment to determine impact of new emerging trends
4. Don't whip saw the R&D organization with too many large corrections

---

PORTFOLIO PLANNING IN THE MEDICAL DEVICE MARKET

THE SET UP

OK, OK I give up! A number of my colleagues have asked for a lesson relating to building a Product or Technology portfolio. I have been reluctant to write this lesson for a number of reasons. 1) every portfolio planning process needs to be customized to the company and the type of products under development, 2) portfolio planning is very complex, and 3) they need to be preceded by a Corporate Strategic Planning process.

I think the best that I can hope for from this lesson is to identify some common elements of every portfolio plan, define what one is and provide some cautions to take into account as you develop your plan.

WHAT IS A PORTFOLIO PLAN?

Essentially, a product portfolio plan is one that identifies the New Product contribution to the long-term revenue forecast of a company as made by individual product development projects or acquisitions. Typically, you start with either a collection of opportunities that have already been identified or a set of market conditions that the strategic plan wants to leverage. Add in a set of current performing products and a competitive threat matrix, stir all this together and then go crazy.

My preference is to ignore everything that has been done to date and start from the output of the strategic plan and identify the areas for investment. Identify the current products that contribute in those areas, identify unmet customer needs from those areas and identify potential products to resolve those unmet needs, then build the plan from scratch.

The goals of the portfolio plan will be driven off of the corporate strategic plan. Profit, revenue growth, competitive action, leadership, share dominance, access, and discovery are all legitimate goals that can be derived from the strategic plan. In economic speak the Portfolio plan should maximize the combined output, Xp; for the minimum investment Yp; at the lowest risk, β.

In finance we often refer to a balanced portfolio as a goal. I tend to believe that instead of balance one should strive for harmony. Balance is a precise thing, harmony has some freedom around it. The ultimate portfolio will hold many assumptions at multiple levels and we should strive to make it as accurate as possible, but it will never be precise.

No project or combination of projects is/are without risk. All known risks can be managed. Managing risk takes time and money. Risk is a big concept in the medcial device space. So let me be clear, the risk I am talking about is the chance that your total portfolio does not produce your desired outcome, does not meet the needs of the strategic plan and its inherent goals. Lets refer to this risk as β. There are other ways that the concept of risk sneaks into the portfolio plan. Mostly notable as a discount factor for the revenue estimates of each independent opportunity that are ultimately combine to produce the portfolio plan.

THE STEPS IN BUILDING A PORTFOLIO PLAN.

For me:

Step 1   Read and understand the strategic plan. (Pull out the explicit and implicit measurable goals from the plan).

Step 2   Interview all the senior managers that were involved with creating the strategic plan to make sure you have a feel for each of their visions for the portfolio.

Step 3   Create a heat map of market and competitive risk, basically a FMEA assessment of your SWOT analysis that should come from the Strategic plan.

Step 4   Create a matrix of segments that the strategic plan identifies that you want to be in, enter or exit.

Step 5   Survey the clinicians that are the key users or drivers of/in those segments.

Step 6   Identify the opportunities that exist.

Step 7   Have teams create an opportunity assessment for each opportunity.

Step 8   Score each opportunity in terms of it's contribution to the objective for that segment that was identified in the strategic plan.

Step 9   Score each opportunity in how well they reduce risk identified from the heat map.

Step 10   Score each opportunity by the cost of realizing that opportunity.

Step 11 Either use a discount factor to fold in the risk of success or failure of the project (Innovation, core competency, speed, timing, competitive development).

Step 12 Using the four scores force rank the opportunities separately, so that you have a list that is ranked by score 1, score 2, score 3, score 4. Typically, the high impact / low cost ones will be at the top. Those at the bottom of all four scores are usually out. It is the middle ones that require some discussion.

Step 13 Allocate the New Product budget to each of the opportunities and see how far down the list the money will go. Ask two questions if we execute this plan will we achieve the strategic intent of the company? Is our portfolio plan in harmony with our willingness to absorb risk?

Last Step Vet the plan with the bosses, dispassionately.

CAUTIONS

1. The development of a portfolio plan is not an engineering exercise, it is a social-science experiment. An experiment with significant political implication.
2. Each opportunity must be assessed under a strict set of guidelines. Inconsistency in the approach and definitions will invalidate your portfolio plan.
3. Marketing can not do this process alone. It must be a team effort between R&D, NBD, Up stream marketing, finance and operations.
4. Document in a very obvious manner all the assumptions that are used. Independently vet the assumptions to ensure that everyone is OK with the assumptions. If they are not OK with the assumptions, stop and develop a plan to move the assumptions to facts.
5. It will be difficult, but don't take it personally, any of it.
6. If your organization is not willing to allow the time and dollars to develop a great portfolio plan then you are better of getting the most informed opinions in a room and make the call without data, a modified Monte Carlo process.
7. A portfolio plan needs to be reviewed constantly and changed seldom.

WHY DO I NEED A PORTFOLIO PLAN?

The life blood of the medical device market has been a continual stream of new products. In today's environment the commercialization process will require 2-5 years from start to finish. If you don't have a well thought out plan you are already behind the time curve.

At many Med Dev companies the goal is launching a new product every year and a new platform every two-years. If you can accomplish this goal you are on your way to sustained growth, if they are the next right projects. A well thought out portfolio plan will drive your M&A activity as well as R&D. If you, as a Marketing organization have effectively laid out where you need to go to accomplish your new product revenue goals, you put yourself in a leadership position and if done well you are moving your organization to be a market driven organization.

FINAL THOUGHT

A well done product portfolio plan that is in harmony with the strategic plan gets the entire organization on the same page. Having the assumptions well understood and monitored will provide an early warning system if changes are required.

The last thing any organization needs is a whipsaw effect in new product development.

LESSONS

1. Having a portfolio plan is the best way to be intentional with R&D dollars

2. If possible keep it simple and transparent

LESSON 33

GOALS AND OBJECTIVES IN PRODUCT PORTFOLIO PLANNING FOR THE MEDICAL DEVICE MARKET

THE SET UP

This lesson is number three in a series of lessons related to Product Portfolio Planning (PPP). Once you have the market risks identified and scored [from the previous lesson] you must then set a revenue goal. This lesson will deal with revenue goal setting and R&D budget setting. These three elements make up the end game for your product portfolio plan. As a reminder the goal of the PPP is to hit target revenue, at target cost levels, with risk that is harmonized with your risk tolerance profile.

PPP GOALS

The source of these Product Portfolio Goals (PPG) should come from a strategic plan (SP) that matches the time frame of the Product Portfolio Plan. If there isn't a SP, then the source of your goals needs to be the CEO, President or VP of Global Marketing.

For larger corporations there will most certainly will either be a SP or a policy intention. Something to the effect that by 20XX, XX% of our revenue will be provided by products launched within the last 5 years. Not too difficult to get to a number.

ILLUSTRATION

So lets say that your company launched their first product in 2000 and in it's first year it produced $20 million in sales. You had a steady release of new products and achieved $500 million by 2005. You had nothing in the R&D pipeline and there were significant shifts occurring in the market with innovation, competition and consolidation. Your CEO announces at a staff meeting that you need a continuous flow of new product introductions such that you achieve $750 million in profitable revenue by 2013.

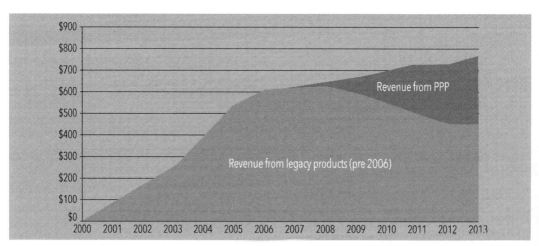

You get back to your desk and do some quick calculations and produce this chart.

You realize that you need $250 million dollars of revenue output from this new PPP within the next 7 years. It takes between 2-5 years to commercialize a product.

In that same staff meeting the CEO indicated that he was willing to invest more than the industry average to achieve that goal. You know from a industry survey and quick review of the competitors Shareholder reports that, on average, companies invest 7-10% on R&D. Taking your CEO at his word it looks like you would have 12% of revenue to invest each year. As sales continue to grow the R&D budget would grow in real dollars as well.

You are feeling a little better now. You know the revenue goal, you know the typical turn time for product development (based on the performance of the nine products that you have launched so far).

BUT WHICH INVESTMENTS?

Where do you place the $60M worth of R&D dollars to guarantee that you reach $750M in revenue? There are two approaches to determine this list of development projects. Top-down or Bottom-up. I suppose there is a third, which is a combination of the two.

For me, an environmental scan of your market is in order. As a quick starting point a Monte Carlo approach to determine the risks and opportunities in the market (as described in the most recent lesson). If there is a recent strategic plan (SP) document you could start there to discover the growing segments and review the SWOT anaylisis. If there isn't a SP, start from scratch.

In parallel, you take a look at what is being worked on in R&D currently. You discover that there are currently 18 projects under development. It appears that in the absence of an agreed to PPP every pet project has emerged and has been funded. This is natural and is exactly why you need a portfolio plan.

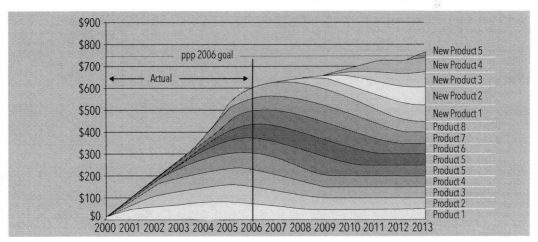

SO YOU ASK YOURSELF HOW MANY PROJECTS SHOULD YOU HAVE?

You do a bit more analysis of the current performance of your products and project that same level of performance forward and you see from your chart that you need around five. You feel that you have a good start but realize that you are going to need a group effort to actual develop the plan. You report out your findings to the CEO and are asked to share your finding with the general staff next week. You do. The CEO then announces that you are now in charge of developing the PPP and that everyone is expected to provide their full cooperation.

The following week you get your team together, R&D, NBD, Finance, Marketing and Operations. The big realization that comes out of the organizing meeting are three very fundamental issues. First, that the market has been shifting for a long time, very slowly and now that you stop to look at the impact of those changes they look huge. Secondly, that R&D does not have a standardized method for comparing projects. If you are going to make a decision about which current and future projects to fund, it is critical that you have a very consistent way for comparing them. Third, that none of the 18 projects are fully funded or are driving toward a commercialization date.

So NBD and marketing head off to get a handle on the market and the market trends. R&D, finance and Ops head off to develop a method to compare projects (investments). You have all agreed to comeback in two-weeks with a status report. Meantime you have one of your Product Directors working on the market Risk assessment.

Two weeks later you gather again and there is good progress. R&D, Finance and Ops have come up with a model that scores cost, time, head count, technical risk, and capability. What they have not yet factored in are revenue potential, profitability, market acceptance risk and commercialization costs.

Marketing and NBD report back that they have priced out several market

R&D VARIABLES	MARKET VARIABLE
• Utility delivered to end user	• Unmet market need
• Development cost	• Revenue potential
• Time to regulatory clearance	• Profitabilty (price target)
• Head count requirements	• Market acceptance
• Technical capabilities	• Commercialization costs
• Technical risk	• Time to commercialize
DISCOUNT FACTOR DUE TO COMBINED CONFIDENCE OF SUCCESS	

research projects that would provide all the information they need. The price and lead time seem reasonable for the need, however there is no allocated budget to cover the $2M dollars and the six-month time line seems too long for the sense of urgency the CEO has around this project.

You assign a second Product Director to work with R&D and Finance to round out the balance of the project assessment method. You and NDB develop a survey (discussion guide) and make appointments with ten key opinion leaders, luckily 8 are attending a conference over the week-end and you will be there. While at the conference you speak with a total of 20 physicians and have what you think is a pretty good handle on the market needs.

Your next meeting with the extended team is a half day working session. Everyone reports out their findings. You now have a method for comparing projects, you have a feel for the market trends, you have a risk map that was developed [which your CEO, and all geographic experts, internal experts and two external market expert have scored].

During the half-day session you develop a table that organizes all the relevant information.

RISK or TREND	SOURCE	IMPORTANCE / SIZE	PROJECT	OUTCOME

This chart is critical. It will provide a narrative surrounding the "as is condition" of your portfolio. The format and style is less important that the content. For me I would use 11x17 paper in profile.

What should become obvious from this charting process is the list of projects that are ongoing in R&D that have no bearing on the market reality that you are dealing with. Also, where the large holes are that need to be filled.

THE NEXT STEPS

1. Envision projects that would fill the holes
2. Re-score the Market Risk Assessment based on these new projects
3. Re-score the projects using the consistent methodology
4. Rank the projects using 1) discounted revenue potential, 2) pay back period 3) positive impact to market risk reduction. You can also use NPV or IRR calculations.

CHART THE RANKINGS BY PROJECT

PROJECT NUMBER	PROJECT NAME	EXPECTED REVENUE	PAYBACK PERIOD	RISK REDUCTION IMPACT	COMBINE RANK SCORES	COMBINED RANKINGS
1		2	3	1	6	1
2		3	5	4	12	2
3		5	7	6	18	3
4		1	2	3	6	1
n						

Prioritize the list of projects by combined rankings and then pour the R&D budget over the top letting it rain down until it is gone.

◀ Investment Funds

◀ Projects

HINT: Never partially fund a project. Dry pancakes are just not satisfying.

LESSONS

1. Fully fund a project or don't fund it at all
2. It is OK to phase projects with funding in the light of uncertainty
3. Always try to take a futuristic perspective, these portfolio plans have to be durable

ABOUT THE AUTHOR

Tim Walker has been successfully commercializing new products in the Medical Device Market for over 35 years. His natural generosity manifests in his desire to coach and mentor young marketing talent. Through his blog, *Insights* for Medical Device Marketers [medicaldevicemktgblog.com] he communicates his experiences by telling real life stories in the hopes that those entering this profession won't have to repeat the learnings of those who have gone before them.

Tim's experience spans the full gambit on several dimensions of the market. From Fortune 50 companies [J&J, Baxter, 3M] -to- start-ups [Anecare Labs, MedQuest Products] and everywhere in between [Thoratec, Merit, Medex]. From Class III devices –to- Class I devices. From Cardio-Thoracic surgeons to dialysis nurses. From $125,000 –to- $15 price points. From capital equipment –to- single use disposables. From Global Vice President of Marketing –to- Marketing coordinator. From QA –to- R&D –to- Marketing –to- Professional Services and back –to- Marketing where he has continue his career for the last 25 years. For more details visit www.theexperiagroup.com or see Tim's LinkedIn profile.

Tim holds a Certificate in Advance Marketing Strategy from The Ross Business School, The University of Michigan; an Executive MBA from The Eli Broad Graduate School of Management, Michigan State University; and a BBA in Management and Marketing from Eastern Michigan University. He is now the owner and principal strategist for The Experia Group®, LLC.

ABOUT THE EXPERIA GROUP®, LLC.

The Experia Group was founded based on the belief that of the thousands of medical device companies in the US there are times when Experience and Expertise are needed that are just not available. The Experia Group can provide extra bandwidth or depth to any medical device commercialization effort.

We work in many ways, but by far our most rewarding method is when we combine mentoring and coaching with a strong emphasis on getting the work done. We would rather work with you and leave behind an elevated capability when the work is finished.

The Experia Group is getting ready to launch a web-based mentoring program called ⊕INSIGHTS. The vision is to recruit medical device marketers to join in a mentoring program that involves group video conferences, 1:1 time with Tim Walker and annual conferences all intended to build a community of like minded professionals all focused on supporting each other's success.

Stay tuned for the launch of this exciting new concept.

Tim

Made in the USA
Columbia, SC
24 November 2018